Advance Praise for
Our Daily Biscuit

"Todd and Michelle have delivered a heartwarming collection of devotions that will satisfy your soul—like a hot plate of biscuits!"
—Dr. Robert Jeffress, First Baptist Church, Dallas

"This book is a buttermilk biscuit for the soul."
—Governor Mike Huckabee

"Southerners are known for many things. Their charm. Soft drawls. Fine cooks. Amazing (and sometimes over the top) stories. And a deep and abiding faith. Todd Starnes and Michelle Cox feature all of those things in their new devotional book, *Our Daily Biscuit: Devotions with a Drawl*. (Even if you aren't from the South, they'll still welcome you into the family.) So pick up a copy today. You'll laugh, wipe tears away, draw closer to God, and even find some recipes from those great Southern cooks. What could be better than that?"

—Brian Bird, Co-Creator and
Executive Producer of *When Calls the Heart*

"You're gonna love these *Devotions with a Drawl*. Matter of fact, you might 'drool' over them like 'The Swan!' Get yourself a napkin and a cup of coffee and be fed spiritually and emotionally. You might want to grab a biscuit as well."

—Dennis Swanberg ("The Swan"),
America's Minister of Encouragement

"What could be finer than biscuits and gravy? Biscuits and devotions! In *Our Daily Biscuit: Devotions with a Drawl*, Todd Starnes and Michelle Cox share funny and poignant stories about colorful Southern characters, devotions, recipes, prayers, and Bible verses, and then they add a little gravy on top with questions for reflection. I can promise you've probably never read a devotional book quite like this before, but you'll be glad you did (even if you're just a Southern wanna-be)."

—Megan Alexander, National Correspondent
for *Inside Edition*, Author and Mom

"Are you from the South? You'll love this book. Those of you from the North, East, and West will too. Todd and

Michelle bring bursts of side-splitting laughter, tons of out-of-this-world Southern food (yes, there are recipes!) and a whole lot of Jesus in this much-needed devotional. Truly, in this day and time, I can't think of a better combination. I laughed. I snickered—there might have even been a guffaw or two—but mostly, I drew closer to Jesus. I highly recommend this book. And the recipes."
—Lynette Eason, Award-Winning, Bestselling Author of the *Danger Never Sleeps* series

Our Daily Biscuit

Devotions with a Drawl

Todd Starnes and Michelle Cox

A POST HILL PRESS BOOK
ISBN: 978-1-64293-892-0
ISBN (eBook): 978-1-64293-893-7

Our Daily Biscuit:
Devotions with a Drawl
© 2021 by Todd Starnes and Michelle Cox
All Rights Reserved

Cover art by Joseph Huntley

All Bible verses were copied and pasted from Bible Gateway.

Post Hill Press
New York • Nashville
posthillpress.com

Published in the United States of America

2 3 4 5 6 7 8 9 10

Dedicated to the dear citizens of Starnes Country for filling our lives with great cheer on the radio.
—Todd

And in loving memory of my sweet Grandpa Haynes. He was a true Southern gentleman whose daily example taught me about life, love, and Jesus.
—Michelle

Contents

Welcome to Our Front Porch

Country is not just a geographic location. It's a state of mind. A shared sense of values like faith and family.

Michelle is from North Carolina, and I'm from Tennessee. But we've met plenty of country folks from places like Chicago and New York City and even San Francisco.

So, what's so special about country folks? Well, I reckon it starts with the people. They greet you with sincere hospitality, soft Southern drawls, and timeless manners.

The children say "Yes, ma'am" and "No, sir" out of great respect and under threat of granny's switch or momma's cast iron skillet.

Country is a place where neighbors lend a helping hand. Whether it's harvesting a crop or raising money for a Little League team or buying groceries for a family on hard times. As a country song writer once crooned, I have "Friends with Tractors."

It's a place where folks still speak to strangers and wave as cars drive down a gravel road. Where gentlemen are still gentlemen and ladies are still ladies. And where hugs are just as plentiful as the Mason jars of sweet tea at a small-town meat-and-three.

If a country lady invites you to partake of dinner at her table, you'd better jump at the chance—because they know how to cook! And somehow, there's always room at that lace-covered table for one more.

Enjoy potato salad. Banana pudding. Cobblers made from peaches picked fresh from the tree. Fluffy biscuits. Crispy fried chicken. Pork tended with love in the smoker. And Granny's famous sweet potato pie. Are you hungry yet?

Drive through the country. Stop and watch farmers on tractors in their fields and families working together in the garden. Visit roadside stands for fresh-picked produce and home-canned fruits, vegetables, and jams made from the bounty of the farm.

Mosey through the back roads of our great nation and discover a genteel, slower pace of life. You'll find majestic blue-ridged mountains. Tranquil meadows filled with wildflowers. Beaches with sugar-white sand. Swamps filled with alligators and mystery. Fields ready for the cotton harvest. Trees draped with Spanish moss blowing gently in the wind like a grandmother's shawl. And forest glades that invite you to enter in and sit a spell.

Pull up a rocking chair or discover the squeak of the swing as families sit on the porch talking and laughing as they string and snap beans, tossing them into a chipped porcelain dishpan handed down from their grandparents.

Enjoy small towns where everybody knows everybody else's business—and often shares it. As a prayer request, of course.

And soak in the countless things that make us love life in the South. Clotheslines with quilts and laundry flapping on the line. Old houses and barns with stories to tell. Sweet honeysuckle on a fence. Climbing roses on garden gates. And the aroma of fragrant lilacs drifting through the kitchen window.

Listen to children laugh as they chase lightning bugs or wade in the creek catching salamanders and crawdads. As they walk barefoot in tender blades of grass and swing far out over the creek on sturdy vines. Cast a fishing line into the pond. Relax and take a few turns on the tire swing hanging from the tree. Or hang out at a Friday night hometown football game.

But the best part about life in the country? There's a deep and abiding faith. You're welcome to worship at little white churches where bells still clang throughout the community, reminding everyone that it's time for church. Stay afterward for gospel singings and potluck dinners on the grounds. Come back for summer revivals and sweet baptisms in the river. And experience God's precious truths that have been handed down from generation to generation—the most priceless gift our ancestors had to leave behind.

That's why we decided to write *Our Daily Biscuit: Devotions with a Drawl*. It's a celebration of faith, family, food, and our Southern heritage. Each chapter features a verse of Scripture, a funny or poignant story about Southern culture—with a devotional tie-in to bless your day or make you think—a prayer, and questions to help you deepen your relationship with God. We've even sprinkled in some recipes from some of those fabulous Southern cooks.

In the South, the welcome mat is always out, so invite your family and friends to share a heaping helping of *Our Daily Biscuit: Devotions with a Drawl*, and then enjoy your day with hearts, souls, and bellies filled to overflowing.

Todd and Michelle

PS: Some names in the following stories have been changed to protect the innocent...and the authors.

Give us this day our daily biscuit.
Matthew 6:11
(Southern paraphrase)

CHAPTER ONE:
Granny Rice's Ham Surprise

The righteous cry, and the Lord hears and delivers them out of all their troubles. The Lord is near to the brokenhearted and saves those who are crushed in spirit. Many are the afflictions of the righteous, but the Lord delivers him out of them all.
Psalm 34:17–19 (NASB)

"God promises that He will never leave us, that He will comfort us, and that nothing will separate us from His love."

The South is famous for wonderful cooking, and Granny Rice was one of the best of those Southern cooks. Friends and family were always excited to receive an invitation to sit around her table and enjoy one of her feasts.

Granny Rice was a sweet lady, a loving mother, and the glue that bound her family together. So you can imagine her joy and relief when her son arrived home safely from his tour of duty in Operation Desert Storm. That mama couldn't wait for the opportunity to fix him a home-cooked meal to welcome him back.

She set about planning a special dinner and purchased one of those round hams in a metal can. It was her first time buying one, and she'd heard you didn't have to take it out of the can to bake it. So she put the canned ham in the oven, set the temperature to the recommended setting, and went outside to visit on the porch with her soldier son and his brother.

One can only imagine the delightful time they had catching up with everything that had been happening in all their lives, enjoying a soft mountain breeze that drifted by as their rockers creaked gently on the porch.

But then their relaxing visit came to an abrupt end when they heard a loud explosion. Her son who'd just returned home from the war thought a bomb had gone off, and he immediately hit the porch floor.

They couldn't imagine what it might have been, but when they walked into the kitchen, they discovered the source of the explosion. The oven door had blown off. The stove burners were sticking up. And the ceiling above the stove was ham-pink.

They never found a scrap of the ham or any of the can, but the story of Granny Rice's ham bomb has become a family classic that has been told many times throughout the years.

Friends, I've never had an exploding ham situation before, but I've had many times when unexpected moments have burst into my life with just that much shock and intensity—and I suspect you have as well.

Job losses and financial hardships can shatter everything we've worked for and put our families in jeopardy, and it's devastating when we get one of those phone calls from the doctor that changes our lives forever.

A prodigal child, a splintered relationship, or the death of a loved one can break our hearts with swift intensity. I'll never forget the shock of the phone call that shared the news of my dad's suicide. That moment was so unexpected.

But the good news—as I learned from experience—is that we never go through those moments alone. God promises that He will never leave us, that He will comfort us, and that nothing will separate us from His love. And those stories of God's faithfulness? Well, they for sure will become family classics that we can tell numerous times throughout the years.

Father, I'm so grateful that when those unexpected moments slam into my life and take my breath away, that You are there with me. The precious promises in Your Word bring me hope and comfort. So many times, when the tears have overwhelmed me, I've felt Your love wrap around me, comforting me like a warm blanket around my shoulders. You are a faithful God, and I can never thank You enough for always being just what I need. Amen.

A LITTLE Gravy ON TOP

1. Granny Rice's ham bomb was totally unexpected. What are some unexpected moments that have happened in your life? What did you learn from them?

2. What are some ways that God has comforted you during difficult times? Spend some time thanking Him for always being there for you.

3. What are some Bible verses that ministered to your heart when you needed them?

4. What are some of the stories you can tell about God's faithfulness? Have you told your loved ones about those moments? Your children need to hear those stories.

5. Take a few minutes today to call, email, or write someone to encourage them as they go through unexpected circumstances.

CHAPTER TWO:
The Long Arm of the Law

Therefore, to him who knows to do good and does not do it, to him it is sin. James 4:17 (NKJV)

Bad decisions never affect just one person. When you make a decision to do the wrong thing, it always impacts the lives of others.

I didn't know about my husband's arrest record until long after we were married. Paul's life on the wrong side of the law began early. His family lived across the street from the elementary school. On summer days, he and his brothers loved spending time on the playground, swinging from the monkey bars and flying high in the sky on the swings. That was back in the era when few folks in the South locked their doors, and it was safe for kids to play throughout the neighborhood.

Paul's mom tried hard to be a good parent. She kept her children faithfully in church, teaching them about the Bible and praying for them, but sometimes despite our best efforts, children just go astray. And that's what happened to Paul, his brothers, and some neighborhood kids on the day of the great school caper, when they went in through an unlocked window and vandalized the building.

The long arm of the law caught up with them quickly, and they ended up going to court to stand before a judge. This might be a good point for me to mention that Paul was just three years old at the time. The judge looked at him and said, "Little man, I'm going to give you a lollipop and send you home." The rest of the boys were duly punished, and all of them grew up to become law-abiding citizens.

Paul married me, became a great dad for our sons, and started a contracting business. He hadn't thought about his life on the wrong side of the law in years—until he went to estimate a job for a client and discovered the man had been one of his partners in crime at the school-house all those years before.

The two reminisced about that schoolhouse moment, and then the man shared some information that Paul hadn't known before. He said, "You know how we got caught, don't you?" Paul replied that he didn't. The man contin-ued, "Well, Philip (Paul's brother who was about six at the time of the school incident) had just learned to print his name, and he wrote 'Philip Cox' on all the blackboards."

I'm sure glad those boys got their act together before they became grown-ups. I don't think they would have made good criminals.

Those little boys made a bad decision, but we adults often make bad decisions as well—and sometimes those choices can haunt us for the rest of our lives. Just as Paul's mom had to go to court with her boys, we're often not the only ones impacted by our wrongdoing. And it's not fun when God's long arm of punishment is extended to us.

But just as that judge had mercy on a little boy named Paul, God has mercy and grace waiting for us—if we're willing to turn from our wrongdoing. But by far, the wisest choice for all of us is to never make that bad decision in the first place.

Dear Lord, I mean to do good, but so often I make wrong decisions and then I bear the consequences. I don't want to grieve You, so keep me close to You. Give me a heart that's tender toward You. Remind me that others are watching and that my actions can harm those I love. Thank You for Your grace and mercy and for Your willingness to forgive me. Amen.

A LITTLE Gravy ON TOP

1. Paul and his brothers made a bad decision—but they learned their lesson. What was a bad decision you made, and what did God teach you from that experience?

2. The boys who were old enough to understand that they'd done wrong were punished. God punishes us as well when we make bad decisions. Why does He do that?

3. Let's be honest—sometimes we do unwise things without even thinking. How can you guard your heart so that you won't disappoint God?

4. When those little guys broke into that school and damaged it, it affected them, but it also impacted the lives of others. Think about how you're living each day. Is your example drawing people to God or is it leading them away from Him?

5. God is so gracious to forgive us when we confess our wrongdoings. Are you as gracious about forgiving others? Can you think of someone you need to forgive?

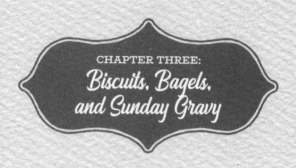

CHAPTER THREE:
Biscuits, Bagels, and Sunday Gravy

A new command I give you: Love one another. As I have loved you, so you must love one another.
John 13:34 (NIV)

"There's no doubt our gravy recipes may be slightly different, but I discovered something that afternoon in Brooklyn—there is one common ingredient that we share—love. And when it comes to God's love, we can share that with everyone, knowing that it will always be more special than even biscuits and Sunday gravy."

I am a true son of the South. I like my tea sweet, my chicken fried, and my biscuits buttered. So you can imagine the culture shock when I moved to New York City, where the tea is unsweetened, the chicken is baked, and the biscuits are called bagels. I stood out like a cheeseburger at a vegan convention.

New York City is truly an amazing metropolis with wonderful people and culture and food. I was introduced to things like pastrami on rye and Nathan's hot dogs. My colleagues at Fox News even got me to eat a bagel—once. Although, I took a pass on the schmear. (I'm a Baptist.)

But even though the Big Apple is the culinary capital of the world, they still haven't figured out Southern cooking. A few years ago, I was on Amtrak's Acela Express heading toward Washington, D.C. when the steward offered me a biscuit breakfast. I gladly accepted his offer and dreamed of a hot, fluffy buttermilk biscuit slathered in real butter and a dollop of elderberry jam. Instead, he served me a "British" biscuit—wrapped in plastic. I nearly broke a tooth. It was a glorified teething cookie.

The city is also home to restaurants serving what they call, "new Southern cuisine." I've discovered that many of these establishments are run by chefs who don't know a turnip green from a mustard green. They're doing stuff to catfish and butter beans that the good Lord never intended.

But there is one commonality between country folks and city folks—Sunday dinner. Oh, it's quite a grand affair north and south of the Mason–Dixon line.

Years ago we would pile into the Oldsmobile after church and head over to Mema's house for a bountiful feast—roast beef, mashed potatoes, and of course, plenty of delicious biscuits and gravy. So you can imagine my delight when a member of my church in New York City invited me over for "Sunday Gravy." Praise the Lord and pass the biscuits, I could barely concentrate on the sermon.

Her Italian-American grandmother greeted me at the door with a bear hug. "Come," she said. "I make you a plate with extra gravy."

I must confess to being a bit bewildered when she brought out a plate piled high with pasta and meatballs. "Where's the gravy?" I asked my friend.

She looked over with a smile and pointed at the meatballs smothered in sauce. "That's what we Italians call gravy," she said. "Sunday Gravy." I dipped the Italian bread into the gravy and commenced speaking in tongues. Mamma Mia! She topped off the meal with banana pudding cheesecake followed by a very long nap.

There's no doubt our gravy recipes may be slightly different, but I discovered something that afternoon in Brooklyn—there is one common ingredient that we share—love. And when it comes to God's love, we can share that with everyone, knowing that it will always be more special than even biscuits and Sunday gravy.

Father, various areas of our country and our world are filled with traditions that are different from ours. There are other languages, unusual foods, exotic cultures, and even a variety of skin colors. But the one thing that can bind us together is love. Your love, Lord, given freely to all who will accept it. Make me a bearer of Your love to everyone with whom I come in contact. Help them to see Jesus in me, and help the love of God to bind our hearts together and heal our world. Amen.

A LITTLE Gravy ON TOP

1. God tells us that we should love others as He loves us. What do you think that means?
2. There's a definite lack of love in our world today. How can you share God's love with others?
3. How does love bind your heart to others?
4. There are no strings attached to God's love. It's freely given to anyone who will accept it. Have you accepted God's love, and do you have a personal relationship with Him? If not, today would be the perfect time to do that.
5. How can God's love (and your love) make a difference in our communities, country, and world? And what can you do to help?

Mema's Chicken Divan

(From the kitchen of Lucile Starnes)

1½ pounds broccoli, cut into bite sized pieces
3 cups cooked chicken breasts, diced
1½ cups shredded cheddar cheese, divided
½ cup milk
⅔ cup sour cream
1 can cream of mushroom (or cream of chicken) soup
½ teaspoon garlic powder
½ teaspoon onion powder
½ teaspoon dry mustard
½ teaspoon black pepper
¼ teaspoon seasoning salt
½ cup butter, melted
1 cup breadcrumbs

Preheat the oven to 400°. Bring a large pot of water to boiling. Add the broccoli. Cook for about 2–3 minutes or until crisp-tender; drain well.

In a medium-sized bowl, combine 1 cup of the cheddar cheese, milk, soup, sour cream, and seasonings. Mix well, and then stir in the broccoli and diced chicken. Spread into a 9x13-inch baking dish or a 3-quart casserole dish that has been coated with cooking spray. Top with the remainder of the cheese.

Mix the butter and breadcrumbs together in a small bowl and then sprinkle over the chicken mixture. Bake for about 18–20 minutes until the mixture is bubbly and hot and the crumbs are lightly browned.

CHAPTER FOUR:
Onion Rings, Sweet Tea,
and Jesus

...for the joy of the Lord is your strength.
Nehemiah 8:10 (KJV)

When our lives are filled with the sweetness of Jesus, it can't help but overflow into the lives of those around us.

Sometimes blessings arrive unexpectedly—but I certainly didn't expect to find one in the middle of a bustling burger joint. My husband and I had traveled to another state on business, and while we were there, we went to one of those classic old Southern restaurants that's built a reputation for serving consistently great food.

We've eaten at this place countless times over the last twenty-five years. The diner is famous for its sweet tea and plates heaped high with oversized chili cheeseburgers and crisp Vidalia onion rings. Guests go through the line, that usually stretches out the doors, and then carry their food to one of the dining rooms scattered throughout the building.

With everyone caught up in enjoying their meal, there usually isn't any interaction between guests at other tables or with the attendant assigned to the room. Not usually. But that day was different.

The attendant was one I'd never seen before. When we carried our trays into the room, she greeted us with a wide smile and a, "Well, hey, sugars! Come on in. I hope you're having a *good* day."

For the entire time we ate our meal, she was in constant motion throughout the room, restocking supplies, wiping off tabletops, and greeting everyone with a warm welcome. Guests usually clear their plates and trash from the tables at this restaurant, but on this day, whenever someone started to do that, the attendant would say, "Honey, you go on and enjoy your day. I'll take care of that."

Her cheerfulness was infectious, and I noticed customers smiling at other diners while they watched her work. And then she started singing while she cleared tables, the rich sound of a hymn drifting through that dining area.

That normally loud room filled with dozens of people became as quiet as church on Sunday morning. Through a haze of tears, I looked around that large space, observing the touched expressions on every face.

That precious attendant could have easily been soured on life. Years of tough times were etched into her face. Some of her teeth were missing. Her clothes were neat and clean but ill-fitting and well-worn. One didn't have to look at her for long to know that this lady hadn't had an easy life.

Instead of griping and complaining while she worked a minimum wage job, this precious lady overflowed Jesus, filling that dining room with the sweet aroma of His presence and preaching a sermon through her life.

I don't know that I've ever seen a lovelier visual of the transformation an attitude can make. And I don't think that I've ever had a more perfect example of the difference one person can make when she's so filled with the sweetness of Jesus that she just can't keep it in. Imagine how our world might change if more of us lived like that.

Onion rings, sweet tea, and Jesus. Thank you, precious lady, for that oh-so-beautiful blessing.

Father, that dining room attendant was so full of You that she overflowed into the lives of everyone in that room. That's what I want for my life. Don't ever let me forget the importance of living for You, even in the little moments. Make me mindful of the fact that others are often watching, and that my attitude and example can either draw them to You or it can send them in another direction. Amen.

A LITTLE Gravy ON TOP

1. I didn't expect to cry over my dinner, but that lady so touched my heart. Can you think of a moment when God sent an unexpected blessing like that to you? What did you learn from the experience?

2. That attendant's joy was contagious. What do others see when they look at you? Are you sharing the joy of Jesus, or do they see a grump who is unkind and irritable?

3. It was evident that the attendant's life wasn't easy, yet her attitude was amazing. What kind of attitude do you have when times are hard or when you encounter difficult circumstances?

4. The attention of everyone in the dining room was drawn to that sweet lady as she sang hymns. They came hungry for food. They left hungry for God. All because one person lived her faith in front of them. How could you do something like that?

5. Sometimes we forget that our lives preach sermons. What would folks see and hear if they spent an hour around you?

CHAPTER FIVE:
Fancy Dancing and Unexpected Guests

But I am afraid that as the serpent deceived Eve by his cunning, your thoughts will be led astray from a sincere and pure devotion to Christ.
2 Corinthians 11:3 (ESV)

"Friends, we get in trouble when we listen to others instead of listening to God. Don't let Satan's whispers lead you away from your devotion to Christ. Train your ears to listen only to Jesus—because His words will always be for your good."

Most Southerners don't like snakes. A few crazy ones do, but we mostly stay far away from them in case their slithery friends might be loose. Just saying.

A six-foot snake once hung from top to bottom of my storm door. That bad boy received an instant eviction order. It was him or me. I won.

When a friend discovered a big snake in his yard, he remembered hearing that if you grab their tail and whip them around over your head, it will kill them. So my friend grabbed the snake's tail and gave it a mighty swing. There was just one problem, though. He lost his grip while the snake was overhead, and it came down and landed around his neck. Some fancy dancing ensued that day.

But Jim Gatling's story tops them all. Jim had watched TV until 2:30 one night. After everything was turned off, he headed to bed, guided by the night lights he has in every room so he can see in the dark. As he got to his bedroom door, Jim was greeted by the biggest snake he'd ever seen.

He jumped backward with the quickness of an Olympic gymnast, hit his shoulder on the hall door, fell, and then scrambled to get back on his feet. The snake was headed straight toward him! Jim started down the hall for his phone to call the police. Surely they would come shoot the snake. But the phone was on the bedside table—and the snake was between him and the phone.

Jim turned the hallway light on and started creeping down the hall next to the vent. The heat came on, made some noise, and sucked his pajama bottoms into the vent. Jim just knew he was a goner. He screamed so loudly he scared himself, fell into a table, and retreated before it dawned on him what had happened.

He went back to see where the snake was, because if he couldn't find it, it was for certain he had to move. He quietly reached around and flipped the light switch, peeked in, and there it was: the *belt* he'd accidentally knocked off the bed that morning when he changed clothes. Sweet mercy, y'all, that was a close one.

There's another snake we need to watch out for. A dangerous one whose goal is to destroy us: Satan. The Bible calls that snake a serpent, and in the Garden of Eden, he used his wiles to get Eve in trouble.

The serpent actually quoted God's words to Eve, and he twisted them just enough to make Eve believe him. She and Adam went from living in a perfect world to hiding in shame, being cursed, and discovering they'd messed up their relationship with God.

Friends, we get in trouble when we listen to others instead of listening to God. Don't let Satan's whispers lead you away from your devotion to Christ. Train your ears to listen only to Jesus—because His words will always be for your good.

Lord, I so often listen to the wrong voices—especially that of the serpent named Satan. He's cunning, and he tempts me where he knows I'm vulnerable. Close my ears to his lies. Father, help me to listen only to Your voice. Keep my thoughts on You, because I'll never get into trouble if I'm chasing after You with all my heart. And while you're at it, send the serpent an eviction notice—because I only want You in my life. Amen.

A LITTLE
Gravy
ON TOP

1. Why did Eve believe the serpent's lies and how did he lure her to do the wrong thing and directly disobey God?
2. What consequences did she and Adam face because they listened to Satan (the serpent), believed his lies, and directly disobeyed God?
3. How can allowing Satan to lead your thoughts astray impact your devotion to Christ?
4. You know God wants what's best for you, so why do you sometimes listen to other voices instead of His?
5. How can you help others to avoid the serpent's lies—lies that will destroy them or mess up their lives?

CHAPTER SIX:
Granny's Cast Iron Skillet

*Therefore if anyone cleanses himself from
the latter, he will be a vessel for honor, sanc-
tified and useful for the Master, prepared for
every good work.*
2 Timothy 2:21 (NKJV)

"Sometimes God places us into the hot ovens of hardship, through times when we don't understand what He's doing. But after we've withstood the heat, He can use our lives for Him."

I laughed when I saw a Facebook post where my friend ranted because his brother had put his cast iron skillet in the dishwasher. To say he was unhappy was an understatement. (Thankfully, no brothers were harmed in the telling of this story.) But I understood why my friend was so upset. His grandmother had given that skillet to him, and he'd babied it for years. Cast iron is usually handled with care—and would *never* be put in the dishwasher. Especially a cast iron skillet that had sentimental value to it.

In many Southern homes, cast iron skillets have been handed down from one generation to the next. They've been a cherished cooking implement since back in pioneer days, and few old-fashioned grannies below the Mason–Dixon line would be found without one or two of them in their kitchens.

Most of them would swear by the fact that food tastes better when cooked in a cast iron skillet. And judging by the pans of golden cornbread, crispy fried chicken, and other culinary delights that I've sampled from those pans, I'd have to agree wholeheartedly.

A new skillet requires some care, though. It has to be seasoned. The seasoning process affects its durability, and those pans that are treated right will last a lifetime.

To season a new pan, the cook starts by washing, rinsing, and then drying it. The next step is to take a paper towel or cloth and add a thin layer of vegetable oil or melted shortening to the inside and outside of the pan, and to then place it upside down in a hot oven and bake it for an hour. Reapplying a little oil after each use will keep the skillet in great shape for years of repeated use.

If you stop and think about it, caring for cast iron skillets is much like caring for our spiritual well-being. When Jesus comes into our hearts, the first step is to have Him wash away the dirt from our lives. And then begins the process where He seasons us with His Word through regular conversations with Him.

Sometimes God places us into the hot ovens of hardship, through times when we don't understand what He's doing. But after we've withstood the heat, He can use our lives for Him. Then He takes His loving hand of grace and carefully keeps conditioning us so that we'll be ready whenever He wants to use us.

I want God to season me. I want to be durable, and I want my love for Him—and my usefulness to Him—to last a lifetime. And then hopefully, after I've spent enough time coming into contact with Jesus, I'll soak up enough of Him that I can flavor the lives of others.

A well-conditioned iron skillet. A well-conditioned iron faith. Let's keep both of them ready to use.

Lord, my life is much like that iron skillet—sometimes rusty, and always in need of care. I want You to season me so that I'm ready for You to use me. Clean the places that need to be cleaned. Help me to be consistent about caring for my soul. Help me to stand strong when I face those hot ovens of hardship. Make me durable for a lifetime and help me to hand those life lessons down to future generations. Amen.

A LITTLE Gravy ON TOP

1. That grandmother handed down her cast iron skillet to her grandson, and it's a treasure to him. What would you like to pass down to a future generation spiritually?

1. Cast iron skillets require consistent care or they will rust and become unusable. Our souls are the same way. What can you do to stay in good condition for serving God?

1. One of the first steps in seasoning an iron skillet is to clean it well. Are there things in your life that you need to clean so that God can use you?

1. Cast iron skillets are often placed inside a hot oven—and sometimes it feels like we're in a fiery oven of hardship as well. God has a purpose for those moments. They're for our good instead of to harm us. What has He taught you during those times?

1. Cast iron skillets sit in the cabinet waiting to be used. Have you told God that you're available for Him to use you? Today would be the perfect time to do that.

Vera Clement's Bipartisan Cornbread

(Shared by Sarah Cannon)

Sarah's late Aunt Vera (twin sister of Velma Haley of funeral pie fame) had quite a reputation for the cornbread she whipped up in her iron skillet. Whenever you showed up at her house, she'd serve you a Southern feast, and her cornbread, mustard greens, and fried chicken were almost always on the menu.

Like most Southern women, Vera could solve most of the world's problems while sitting at her table enjoying a hot meal.

When Sarah was a little girl, her Aunt Vera taught her to make her famous cornbread, so Sarah could enter it in the Mid-South Fair cooking contest. Sarah says, "She went through each step of the recipe with me, and then she gave me her iron skillet—a prized gift from one generation to the next." Sarah didn't win a ribbon that year, but she finally perfected Aunt Vera's recipe.

Years ago, Sarah worked for Jeff Sessions, the Republican senator from Alabama. And when Mrs. Sessions learned of the cornbread dish, she asked Sarah for the recipe and it quickly became a family favorite.

Each member of the U.S. Senate hosts a bipartisan Thursday lunch group where they feature food from their home state. Sarah is sure that Aunt Vera would have been proud to know that her cornbread was part of that menu when Senator Sessions hosted it.

What a blessing it would be if that cornbread recipe helped to bring members of the United States Senate together so some world problems could be solved.

    1 cup of cornmeal (home grown is best)
    ½ cup of self-rising flour
    1½ teaspoons of salt
    1 teaspoon of baking powder
    ⅓ cup of cooking oil
    1 cup of milk
    pinch of sugar
    3 tablespoons of cooking oil

Preheat the oven to 475°. Mix the dry ingredients in a bowl. Add the oil, milk, and sugar; mix well. Coat the iron skillet with cooking spray, and then put 3 tablespoons of oil in the skillet. Pour the batter in and cover the batter with the excess oil. Bake for 20–25 minutes or until golden brown.

CHAPTER SEVEN:
Hairspray, Beehives, and Blue-Haired Grannies

For I know the plans I have for you," declares the Lord, "plans to prosper you and not to harm you, plans to give you hope and a future."
Jeremiah 29:11 (NIV)

"We can count on God to stick closer to us than that hairspray stuck to those beehive hairdos."

Many years ago, if you wanted to know what was happening in most Southern towns, you didn't need to read the newspaper. You just had to hang out at the neighborhood beauty shop. Why, you could learn more in two hours there than you could in a month of newscasts.

In that hotbed of hairspray activity, hair was teased a foot high to make a beehive hairdo, gray-haired grannies got a rinse that sometimes gave their hair a blue tint, matrons left with freshly washed and styled hair for church on Sunday morning, and—occasionally—some mischief was hatched.

A hair stylist remembers a moment from back then, one that still makes her laugh when she thinks of it. She worked with another beautician (we'll call her Helen) who went to the break room with her pack of cigarettes every chance she got. One day, she rolled a perm for a client and then went to the back to enjoy a smoke break while the client's hair processed.

That's when Helen's coworkers came up with a plan. It was a big joke in the salon that Helen could perm a client's head with just twelve perm rods, leaving huge gaps between each one. So while Helen was in the break room (and with the customer's cooperation), a few of the other hairdressers rolled up the client's cut-off hair onto perm rods and sat them in the gaps between the rods on top of that lady's head.

When their task was completed, they went back to their workstations, pretending to be busy and trying hard to look innocent. When Helen returned, she laid her client back into the sink and began rinsing the perm. Her coworkers will never forget the horrified look on Helen's face when those loose rollers with hair attached fell into the sink. At least twenty women were in the beauty shop that day, and they were all laughing until tears rolled down their cheeks. None of them ever forgot that day or that mischief.

But for the victim of the prank, the moment was so unexpected that she was frozen in shock as she thought she'd done something wrong and caused her customer's hair to fall out. Sweet mercy.

You know what, friends? While this particular unexpected moment had a funny ending, many of ours do not—whether it's a phone call that changes our lives forever, a bad report from the doctor, or the news that we don't have a job anymore. Those are days that we'll also never forget.

But unlike the gaps between those perm rods, there are no gaps in God's grace and mercy. He's never had an unexpected experience. He has a plan for every moment of our lives, and we can count on God to stick closer to us than that hairspray stuck to those beehive hairdos.

Telling about His love and faithfulness would be the perfect story for you to share next time you're hanging out with the girls at the beauty shop.

Lord, those hairdressers had a mischievous plan for their coworker, but I'm so grateful that You have a perfect plan for my life. Thank You for Your grace and mercy that have filled the gaps in my heart. When unexpected moments come, don't let me ever forget that You're a faithful God. Help me to share the story of Your amazing grace whenever the opportunity arises. Amen.

A LITTLE Gravy ON TOP

1. The mischievous hairdressers had a plan for their coworker—one that had a funny ending. God has a plan for our lives, but His has the perfect ending…if we'll let Him be in charge. Have you submitted to God's plan or have you tried to be in control?

2. There were gaps between the perm rods when the hairdresser did them. But when it comes to God's grace and mercy, there are no gaps. Describe a time when God's sweet grace filled the empty places in your life.

3. Those hairdressers will never forget that day in the beauty shop. And there are days in our lives that we'll never forget—whether good or bad. Think of two or three times when God was faithful to provide whatever you needed.

4. Unexpected moments can rock your world. What can you do spiritually to be prepared when those times arrive?

5. The story of that day in the beauty shop has been told many times. Are you as faithful to tell the story of Jesus and how He's changed your life? What keeps you from telling others about Jesus?

CHAPTER EIGHT:
A Southern Boy and His Truck

*You shall love the Lord your God with all
your heart, with all your soul, and with
all your strength.*
Deuteronomy 6:5 (NKJV)

We spend time with and take care of the things that we love.
But the question is: do we show that much care and love
when it comes to serving God?

Southern guys love their trucks—and even some Southern women enjoy driving a big truck. It's part of our culture here below the Mason–Dixon line. I knew that, but I have to admit that I was flabbergasted at the sight in front of me. My youngest son, Jason, was about seventeen at the time. He'd just bought his first truck, and he was excited beyond words. He'd waited a lifetime for this moment. The truck wasn't fresh off the car lot, but it was like new, with no dings or scratches. To put it mildly, the boy was in love.

He couldn't drive the truck for a few days while we waited for the insurance to swap over. His new baby somehow took over my spot in the garage, and Jason spent hours there, vacuuming the carpet, polishing the leather, and cleaning the windows until they sparkled.

He'd start the motor and listen to it purr. He even spent time reading the owner's manual, captivated by every aspect of his new truck.

He pulled the truck into the driveway and washed it three times. And then he towel-dried it, using—as I later discovered—one of my best bath towels. Did I mention he couldn't drive the truck anywhere? When I asked him about it, he said, "It got dusty in the garage." Believe me, that baby gleamed. Every inch was so polished it could have been used for a mirror.

And that led to the moment that made me wonder if I'd really seen what I thought I saw. My son was on his knees on the concrete, his body twisted into the floor of his truck, and he was cleaning the gas pedal. With a *toothpick!*

In disbelief, I said, "Jason Cox, what are you doing?"

He looked at me a trifle sheepishly, and said, "Well, it was dirty, Mom."

All of that from a young man who never noticed the clutter in his bedroom, who never seemed to see the clothes thrown on the floor. Trust me when I say that he'd never paid attention to dirt before—but the difference was that he *loved* that truck.

We laugh, but it's like that for all of us. We spend time with and take care of the things that we love. What if we loved God as much as that teenaged boy loved his first vehicle? Think about what a difference it would make in our lives as Christians if we lavished that much care on our spiritual condition, polishing our hearts until they'd shine for Him.

What if we spent hours reading through the owner's manual—God's Word—hanging onto every verse and thought, interested in even the tiniest of details? What if we took the toothpick of conviction and shone a spotlight on our hearts, carefully removing even the smallest bit of dirt that shouldn't be there?

What if we loved Him like that?

Dear Father, just as that teenaged boy loved his first truck, let me love You with an overwhelming love. Help me to lavish that much care on my heart and life until I can sparkle for You. Let my life reflect Jesus to a world that needs to see Him. And just as Jason spent hours polishing and shining his new vehicle, remind me to spend time in Your Word and in talking with You. Amen.

A LITTLE
Gravy
ON TOP

1. Jason was excited about his new truck. Most of us had that same excitement when we began our relationship with Jesus—but sometimes that fades as time goes by and life gets in the way. What can you do to renew that excitement for serving Him?

2. We take care of and spend time with the things we love. What are some specific steps that you can take to care for your soul?

3. Reading the owner's manual gave Jason valuable information about his truck. How is God's Word the same way?

4. What if God shone a spotlight on your heart to look for unclean and flawed places? What would He find? What areas do you need to address?

5. Jason used a toothpick to clean those barely-visible-to-the-eye specks of dirt from his gas pedal. In the same manner, are you willing to allow God to clean even the smallest stains or wrong-doing from your life?

CHAPTER NINE:
Southern Kindness and Helping Hands

For the good that I would I do not: but the evil which I would not, that I do.
Romans 7:19 (KJV)

We'll never get lost when we follow God's directions. All the instructions for life are laid out there.

Like many Southern congregations, my church takes meals to our members when there's a death or a surgery. Karen is our delivery angel as she takes dinner and love to those who are hurting.

When Ellen faced knee surgery, Karen called her. "Honey, I'll bring dinner by that night for you and your husband."

Since she wasn't sure how long they'd be at the hospital, Ellen said, "Just put the food in the refrigerator. We don't lock our doors, so just go on in. Do you need our address?"

Karen had been there several years before, so she said she remembered where it was. On the day of Ellen's surgery, Karen loaded up the food and left for her delivery. As she started up the steps into Ellen's house, she stopped and asked God to help Ellen make it up the stairs that evening.

Karen's mouth dropped open as she walked into Ellen's house. There were dirty clothes on the floor, soiled dishes, and clutter. The place was a wreck.

The mess was unexpected, but Karen couldn't let Ellen come home to that after surgery. She put the food into the refrigerator, rolled up her sleeves, and soon the house was sparkling clean and ready for Ellen's recuperation.

But that night, Ellen called. "Karen, I thought you were bringing dinner."

"It's in your refrigerator."

When Ellen replied that the refrigerator was empty, Karen said, "Honey, I put it there. I even stood on your steps and prayed that you'd be able to get up them okay."

And that's when Ellen said, "Karen, we don't have steps on our house."

Yes, Karen had taken the food to the wrong house. Can't you imagine the stunned expressions of those neighbors who arrived home and discovered a clean house, freshly-folded laundry, and a stocked refrigerator?

Karen's first mistake came when she didn't ask for directions. And that's often where we mess up. We don't spend time in our Bibles. And yet all the instructions for life are laid out there. We don't listen when God whispers to our hearts. Shucks, we're usually in such a rush that we couldn't hear Him if He *tried* to talk to us.

Because of the mistake, Ellen's family didn't have dinner when they got home from the hospital. When we mess up, it also affects the lives of others.

Karen had the best of intentions—she just arrived at the wrong house. We often do the same thing spiritually. We make plans. We launch forth with zeal. But are we doing what God wants us to do? Let's ask Him to show us His plans for us—because none of us want to end up with a plan that's gone awry.

Dear Father, Karen meant to do well, but there were consequences when she messed up. Please guide my steps so that my actions don't negatively impact those I love. Remind me that Your directions for my life are always better than my plans. Help me to spend time in Your Word and to pay attention to the wisdom there. Make my heart sensitive to those sweet whispers from You. Amen.

A LITTLE

Gravy

ON TOP

1. Karen tried to provide dinner, kindness, and compassion to Ellen and her family. What can you do to share God's love with someone?

2. Karen had the best of intentions, and most of us mean well when we set out to do something for God. Do you launch out under your own steam or have you asked Him if what you want to do is *His* plan for you?

3. Karen didn't ask for directions and it led to a big mess-up. Can you think of a time when you didn't ask God for direction in your life? What kind of difference does it make when you seek Him first and follow His plans for you?

4. What is the best way to discover God's plans for your life?

5. One of the consequences of Karen's mistake was that Ellen's family didn't receive their dinner. What are the consequences when you make mistakes spiritually?

Nana Sexton's Macaroni and Cheese

(From the kitchen of Jacquie Sexton)

You'll almost always find macaroni and cheese on those big serving tables at a church homecoming, and you can count on it being awesome—and homemade—when a Southern cook is involved.

> 16 oz. small elbow macaroni
> 8 oz. (or more) cheddar cheese
> 1 cup milk
> 5 eggs
> 2 teaspoons butter, cut in pieces

Cook the macaroni according to the package directions; drain well and rinse with hot water. Pour half the macaroni into a 9x13-inch casserole dish that has been coated with cooking spray. Spread half of the cheese (shredded or sliced) over the macaroni. Cover with the second half of the macaroni, and then the remaining cheese.

Mix the milk and eggs until well blended. Pour the mixture over the macaroni and cheese. Dot with the butter pieces. Microwave at full power for 5 minutes; stir. Place in oven and bake at 375° for about 30 minutes or until it starts to brown on top.

*But my God shall supply all your need according
to his riches in glory by Christ Jesus.*
Philippians 4:19 (KJV)

"God whispered to me, 'Do you trust Me like that when it comes to providing for your needs? Haven't I *always* been faithful?'"

One of the best parts of living in the country is that we get to enjoy the wildlife in our area. There's been a wide variety through the years. Paul and I have seen red foxes, gray foxes, wolves, bobcats, pheasants, chipmunks, squirrels, snakes (*not* my favorite), and a variety of birds.

Each summer, we get to watch about thirty baby turkeys as they grow up. One of their parents scared me to death one day when I thought somebody was trying to break down our front door—only to discover that a big turkey had seen his reflection in our storm door glass and was attacking it.

Our neighbors have seen bears. One man opened his front door and discovered a mama and her cubs waiting there. We haven't seen them yet at our house, but Paul did see a bobcat walking down our deck stairs when he returned home one evening. I'm glad I haven't had a face-to-face meeting with Bob or Mama Bear. Through the windows is plenty close for me.

But without a doubt, my favorite visitors are the deer. My husband and I love watching them in the meadow behind our home. There's a peacefulness about them, and sometimes we're treated to watching their little ones as they scamper around while their mama enjoys the salt block we've put out for our deer friends. Paul feeds them each evening, and they've learned to trust him. They know his scent. They know the sound of his footsteps. He can talk to them and they just stand there without fear.

When it gets close to feeding time, we can often see one of the deer standing in the backyard looking at our house with an almost lovesick expression, waiting for Paul to come out with the evening meal.

The deer perk up when they hear him shaking the corn in the bucket, and one of them is so comfortable with him that she will wait until he's within a few feet of her before she dashes into the edge of the woods.

I watched the other night as Paul flung the corn out on the ground for them, and then he turned to walk back to the house. He hadn't taken more than ten steps when they started coming out of the woods to enjoy their meal. Seven of them came to dinner that night and a few turkeys joined them.

As I stood on our deck watching the scene, God whispered to me, "Do you trust Me like that when it comes to providing for your needs? Haven't I *always* been faithful?"

Whew, I have to say that sometimes I haven't. I've gotten in a hurry and tried to fix things myself, and often made a bigger mess of things.

I want to be more like those deer who stand there waiting each day, knowing that their needs will be met—because they can trust the one who cares for them.

Father, help me to wait on You just as those deer wait on their corn each evening, standing there in anticipation, without any doubts. You've always been faithful whenever I've needed You, yet I so often greet You with a lack of trust that You'll care for me or provide for my needs. Help me to trust—even when I can't see the answer. And remind me to share about Your faithfulness with those who need to hear about You. Amen.

A LITTLE Gravy ON TOP

1. The deer have learned that they can trust Paul as he provides their food each day. What are some instances where God has provided for you in the past?

2. The deer are often waiting for Paul when he goes out to feed them. Do you wait for God to provide what you need or do you worry and launch out to fix things yourself?

3. How can not waiting for God cause problems, and why is it always better to wait for Him?

4. Why do you sometimes have trouble trusting God—especially when you don't see an apparent answer?

5. Think of three people who need to hear about how God has been faithful to you through the years. Share your stories with them and then ask those folks how you can pray for them.

CHAPTER ELEVEN:
Revving Motors and Screeching Tires

Behold, I will do a new thing, now it shall spring forth; shall you not know it? I will even make a road in the wilderness and rivers in the desert.
Isaiah 43:19 (NKJV)

"So I finally did what I should have done in the first place: I prayed a sincere and frantic prayer, 'God, get me out of this mess!'"

U s Southern gals can get in a heap of trouble. That trouble found me recently at the outlet mall. I was thrilled to discover that the front parking place was empty—but I realized I'd cut it too close as I pulled in when my back right tire ended up on the approximately ten-inch-high concrete landscaping island. I was so embarrassed.

As I pulled the rest of the way into the space, though, the tire dropped off the side of the island with a thud. I breathed a big sigh of relief. But the 4Runner was crooked, so I thought I'd back up and straighten it. As I did, I realized that when the tire had dropped down, it had wedged against the concrete.

I thought I'd pull up just a bit so I'd be able to maneuver around. And that's when I discovered I had a really *big* problem; there was another piece of concrete at the front of the parking space to keep people from pulling through. And I was wedged between the two places without a speck of room to move.

Yes, folks, I was officially stuck in a parking place.

I pushed hard on the gas pedal as I tried to back up, but the island was too high to get back up on. Thick black smoke from the tire rubbing against the concrete poured into the air while the revving motor, screeching sound, and hot rubber smell caught everyone's attention. I was mortified. Out of my peripheral vision, I could see people standing frozen on the sidewalk as they watched the crazy woman wedged in the parking place.

Sweat dripped down my back as I made multiple embarrassing and unsuccessful attempts to inch forward and backward. It seemed like that went on for days. I did *not* want to call my husband to come get me because I was stuck in a parking place.

So I finally did what I should have done in the first place: I prayed a sincere and frantic prayer, "God, get me out of this mess!" And the next time I tried to pull forward, I could tell I'd found a speck of room. Several attempts later, I was finally able to get out of the parking space.

Sweet friends, I was desperate that day to find a way out of that parking place, and sometimes it's the same way in our lives. We end up in Dead-End Alley, stuck in our circumstances with seemingly no way out.

Are you there today? The good news is that God says we don't have to remain stuck. He promises to do a new thing for us and to make a road in the wilderness. Maybe you need to do what I did that day when I was stuck—cry out to the One who can handle the situation without any problem—even when it involves revving motors, screeching tires, and a frazzled Southern woman.

Father, so often when I'm stuck in the midst of difficult circumstances, I try to solve things myself. And sometimes I forget to pray, to even ask You for help. Remind me to bring my concerns and fears to You, and remind me that true strength lies in You. Thank You for being the God who can handle any situation, who specializes in helping me get out of those circumstances where I see no way out. And thank You for Your patience when I'm a slow learner. Amen.

A LITTLE Gravy ON TOP

1. I did something without paying attention and bore the consequences for it. Can you think of a time when you did something like that spiritually? What did you learn from that situation?

2. I was in too much of a hurry as I pulled into the parking place, and that led to a stressful experience. What can happen spiritually when we're in too much of a hurry, when we move ahead of God?

3. I was stuck—trapped—in that parking place and saw no way out. Have you ever felt that same way because of circumstances in your life? How did God help you?

4. I was so upset over what was happening that day that I forgot to do what I should have done in the first place. I forgot to pray. Why do you think we do that?

5. God promises to do a new thing in our lives and to make a road in the wilderness for us. What new thing would you like for Him to do? Have you prayed about it?

CHAPTER TWELVE:
A Little Farm Girl Shall Lead Them

Those who sow in tears shall reap in joy. He who continually goes forth weeping, bearing seed for sowing, shall doubtless come again with rejoicing...
Psalm 126:5–6 (NKJV)

We'll never reap a harvest for God if we don't plant some seeds of faith.

Drive down most country roads in the South and you'll notice farmers in the fields. It's a peaceful scene to watch as they till the soil, load their crops onto wagons, or cut hay for their cattle. Many of those farms are on family land that has been handed down for generations. You'll often see parents and grandparents in the fields working with their children and grandchildren, teaching them about how to raise cattle, when to plant seeds, when to harvest, and other necessary skills.

My granddaughter, Anna, is eleven, and she's one of those little farm girls. She's already learning the craft of farming—showing pigs and sheep at the state fair, sowing seeds in the garden, and bottle-feeding the baby calves in the barn.

I love that she's acquiring those skills, but even more than that, I love that the family faith is also being handed down to our sweet girl as her parents take her to church, teach her Bible verses, and pray with her and her siblings each evening. And that's where Anna learned a second lesson about planting seeds—spiritual ones.

A while back, Anna and her mama, Lydia, were talking one night at bedtime when the subject of an elderly relative came up. Their family had been praying each night for Uncle Bill to get saved, to find a personal relationship with the Lord. Anna said, "Mama, if he doesn't ask Jesus into his heart, will he go to heaven?" Lydia explained what the Bible says about salvation in John 3:3 (KJV), "Except a man be born again, he cannot see the kingdom of God."

With tears in her eyes—tears for a man she'd never met—Anna replied, "Well, why won't he do it?" Lydia explained that sometimes people harden their hearts. By then, tears were streaming down Anna's face. "Mama, can we go see him tomorrow?"

Lydia looked at Anna, "Are *you* going to talk to him?"

Anna replied, "I will."

Lydia figured she'd forget about it before the next morning—especially since they had a playdate with friends set up—but she was wrong. The first thing Anna said was, "Mama, are we going to see Uncle Bill?" So Lydia, Anna, and Anna's younger twin siblings headed to his house.

They sat on the porch with him. Lydia shared a bit about why they'd come, and then the little ones needed to use the restroom. While Lydia was gone with them, Anna took him by the hand and said, "It's so easy, Uncle Bill. All you have to do is ask Jesus into your heart. Will you do it today?"

When he said no, Anna's little heart was broken—but my sweet farm girl planted some powerful seeds that day. Would we have cared that much?

And that brings me to some important questions: what kind of seeds are *we* planting each day? Will they matter for eternity? And have *you* asked Jesus to come into your heart? It's the most important decision you'll ever make.

Father, a harvest won't occur if we haven't planted any seeds. Just as Anna cared about Uncle Bill, help me to be faithful to plant seeds—to tell others about You. Remind me that there are people around the world who have never heard about You. Make my heart tender, and as you bless me financially, help me to give so that the Gospel can be shared with those who need to hear the message of Jesus. Amen.

A LITTLE Gravy ON TOP

1. The ground has to be prepared before seeds can be planted. How can you prepare so that you will grow and mature spiritually?

2. Crops won't grow unless seeds have been planted—and others won't hear about God unless we tell them. What are some practical ways that you can plant seeds of faith in the lives of others?

3. Anna's little heart was broken because her elderly relative didn't accept Jesus. That day at his house, she whispered and told her mama, "We can't leave until he says yes." When's the last time you shared the good news about Him? When's the last time you wept over someone's soul?

4. Anna urged her mama to take her to see Uncle Bill right away. We have the best news in the world, so why do we put off sharing about our faith?

5. If you stop and think about it, all of us are planting seeds each day. Are you planting seeds that will matter for eternity?

Nana Sexton's
Stuffed Baked Squash

(From the kitchen of Jacquie Sexton)

> 4–6 medium-sized yellow squash
> ½ stick melted butter
> 10–15 saltine crackers, coarsely crushed
> 1 tablespoon finely diced Vidalia onion (or other sweet onion)
> salt and pepper

Bring a large pot of water to a boil. Cut the ends off the squash and place each whole squash into the boiling water. Boil until the squash feels tender when a knife is inserted into the center. (This will take approximately 30 minutes depending on the size of the squash.)

Remove the squash from the boiling water and cut in half lengthways. Scoop out the insides and mash together with the melted butter, the coarsely crushed saltine crackers, and the diced Vidalia onion. Add salt and pepper until well-seasoned. Spoon the mixture back into the shells and place on a cookie sheet that has been lined with foil and sprayed with cooking spray. Bake at 400° until lightly browned (about 10–20 minutes).

CHAPTER THIRTEEN:
Don't Mess with a Southern Lady's Pies

And be kind to one another, tenderheart-
ed, forgiving one another, even as God in
Christ forgave you.
Ephesians 4:32 (NKJV)

"Kindness and respect defuse situations, and even better, they please the heart of God. Do *you* need to take a pie and kindness to someone today?"

There's a bipartisan rule in the Deep South: never question the authenticity of a Southern woman's homemade pie. Ever.

You can debate the merits of cornbread dressing versus chestnut stuffing. You can argue over roasted turkey or deep fried. But it's considered uncouth to suggest a Southern woman would sully the sanctity of the Thanksgiving Day table with a store-bought pie.

And that brings me to one of the most bizarre stories I ever had to report during my time at Fox News Channel. Sarah Huckabee Sanders, the former White House press secretary (and my friend), had been doing some holiday baking, and she posted a picture of her culinary masterpiece on Twitter.

"I don't cook much these days, but managed this Chocolate Pecan Pie for Thanksgiving at the family farm," she wrote. The scrumptious pie stirred the suspicions of CNN political analyst April Ryan, who all but accused the White House press secretary of faking the pie.

"I am not trying to be funny but folks are already saying #piegate and #fakepie. Show it to us on the table with folks eating it and a pic of you cooking it. I am getting the biggest laugh out of this," Ryan tweeted.

Ms. Ryan has some nerve—questioning the authenticity of a Southern woman's homemade pie. She may as well have accused Sarah of bringing store-bought chicken to the Wednesday night church fellowship supper.

I reached out to Sarah, and she assured me that not only did she bake the pie, but it was a recipe handed down from her grandmother. In spite of Ms. Ryan's injurious and slanderous accusations, Sarah offered to bake her a chocolate pecan pie. Ms. Ryan added insult to injury by declining it. "I want to watch you bake it and put it on the table," she tweeted. "But I won't eat it. Remember you guys don't like the press."

My good buddy Mike Huckabee, the former governor of Arkansas, defended his daughter's honor during an appearance on Fox Business Network. And he offered some wise advice to the nation at large.

"Don't ever, and I mean don't ever, mess with a Southern woman and her homemade pies," the governor said. "It is as dangerous as when you hear a Southern woman begin her sentence with 'Bless your heart.' It means you're about to be gutted like a deer, but you just don't know it."

Ms. Ryan's actions highlighted a couple of important things, though. There's a huge need for respect and kindness in our world today. Jesus tells us to be kind to one another, and that's where Sarah provided a lesson to the nation, one she'd learned from godly parents and from years in God's Word. Instead of answering with anger and ugly words, Sarah responded with kindness and even offered to bake Ms. Ryan a pie.

Kindness and respect defuse situations, and even better, they please the heart of God. Do *you* need to take a pie and kindness to someone today?

Father, sometimes people are just downright mean. It feels like they even take pleasure in it. I'm saddened as I watch our culture decline: basic kindness and respect for others is the rarity rather than the norm. Your Word tells us to be kind to others. Help me to be a daily example of that. When others treat me wrong, when they say things that aren't true, and even when they deliberately do things to hurt me, help me to respond with kindness and Your love. Let them see something different in me. Help my life to be a reflection of You. Amen.

A LITTLE Gravy ON TOP

1. Sarah Huckabee Sanders was unjustly accused. It's easy to respond in like manner when people say hurtful things, but she replied with kindness. What can you learn from that?

2. Jesus was treated unkindly by many people, but he always responded with love. How has that love affected your life whenever He's shown undeserved kindness and mercy to you?

3. Why do you think kindness and respect for others is disappearing from our culture? What is the answer for that and how can you be part of the solution?

4. How can kindness and respect defuse ugly situations? Why is it important for us to respond in that manner even when it isn't deserved?

5. Why does it please God's heart when we're kind to others who don't warrant our kindness? And how does it affect you when you respond in the right manner?

*Wait on the Lord; Be of good courage,
And He shall strengthen your heart; Wait, I
say, on the Lord!*
Psalm 27:14 (NKJV)

"Are you in the middle of waiting on God today? Wait on the One who sees the big picture, who always has a purpose in making us wait, and who wants the very best for us—because it's for sure that God's fixes are always **so** much better than ours."

Southern women are often quite resourceful. Give us a challenge, and we'll make it happen. Give us a problem, and we'll fix it. That can be a good thing, but sometimes, well, sometimes things don't go exactly as planned.

When Melissa discovered a one-inch scratch on her car door handle, her fiancé, Brian, told her not to touch it, that he'd fix it. He knew the scratch wasn't deep, so he'd just have to buff it when he returned from his weekend trip.

But Melissa wasn't willing to wait on him to get back because she thought she could fix it herself. That unwillingness to wait led to quite a chain of events.

When Brian returned on Monday, he discovered that the green Honda Civic was now four different colors. Four. With a stunned expression, he asked, "What happened to the car?"

Melissa said, "I didn't want to wait for you to get home, so I tried to fix it myself. I bought a can of the factory green paint at the auto parts store."

After returning to her house that day, Melissa had sprayed the scratch on the door handle. But because the car was twelve years old and the color had faded, the new paint stood out. So she decided to paint the whole door to make it match.

Only, now the door stood out as a different color from the rest of the car. So, trying to get everything to blend, she painted the fender well…and then she painted the hood…and then the passenger side fender well…and then the passenger door.

But then the back doors didn't match. The paint was beginning to run low in the can, so she had the bright idea to paint those doors and feather the paint into the rest of the car. Hence, the four-toned Honda Civic.

And all of that for a one-inch scratch on the door handle.

We laugh at the story, but don't we do exactly that same thing spiritually? We're in the middle of a situation or we have a big dream on our hearts, and we're ready to plow ahead and fix things ourselves. But then God says, "Wait."

On many occasions, we don't wait on Him at all. Other times, we listen and wait, but when we get tired of God not moving in the time frame that we expect, we take things into our own hands. And then—just as Melissa did—we make a giant mess that He has to clean up before He can fulfill the plan that He has for us.

Are you in the middle of waiting on God today? Wait on the One who sees the big picture, who always has a purpose in making us wait, and who wants the very best for us—because it's for sure that God's fixes are always *so* much better than ours.

Lord, I so often take things out of Your hands
and place them into my far-less-capable ones.
I get in a hurry to make things happen, and I
don't wait on You. Remind me that You have
a purpose for the waiting period, and that even
though I don't see things happening, that doesn't
mean that You aren't busily at work on my
behalf. Help me to wait on You so that You don't
have to clean up my messes. Amen.

A LITTLE Gravy ON TOP

1. God knows what to do in our lives, and everything is an easy fix for Him, but we often try to fix things ourselves instead of waiting for Him. Why do we do that?

2. Brian knew that new paint wouldn't match the paint on the twelve-year-old car, but Melissa didn't ask him for wisdom or guidance. That's often our first mistake spiritually. Is there something you need to ask God for guidance about today?

3. Even though Melissa quickly saw that her paint job wasn't going well, she just kept on going. Why are we often so slow to admit that we've made a mistake?

4. We don't want to wait on God for the situations in our lives. What are some reasons why God asks us to wait?

5. When God asks us to wait, it isn't because He doesn't love us. What have you learned from those circumstances?

CHAPTER FIFTEEN:
*A Patchwork
of Memories*

*As one whom his mother comforts,
So I will comfort you…*
Isaiah 66:13 (NKJV)

God's love is like a grandmother's quilt, covering us with comfort and warmth.

Drive through the mountains of North Carolina and you're apt to see colorful quilts hanging in the yards of quaint craft and antique shops. Quilting was a way for women of previous generations to socialize, catch up on what was going on in the community, and often to pray for those who would receive the quilts as gifts. Many young couples were blessed to receive one as a wedding present, something they would treasure forever and pass down through the generations.

The designs were limitless, with squares, circles, triangles, stuffed puffs, and intricate patterns. And I'm in awe of the time it took to make one. The first few steps were coming up with the design, color scheme, and fabrics. The material was meticulously cut into shapes and then thousands of carefully placed stitches—stitches so tiny that you have to bend close to see most of them—joined the pieces together.

They were true labors of love, and many mountain mothers wrapped their little ones in those quilts and rocked them before bedtime or whenever they needed comfort.

I'm thrilled to have some of my grandmother's quilted pieces. Some are in good shape and some are showing the wear and tear of the years, but all are precious as I imagine Granny sitting there for hours, patiently cutting and stitching.

The colors are spectacular, ranging from soft pastels to vibrant tones. As I stroke my hand across the various fabrics, I always wonder if the plaid material was from one of Grandpa's shirts or from one that an uncle wore. Or if the flowered print was from Sunday dresses my mother or aunts wore to church when they were little girls. I imagine family members curled up in those quilts on chilly mountain nights, literally wrapped in love.

I miss my grandparents, and I'd love to have just one more moment to sit in a rocker on the front porch with them. To watch Granny as she quilted. To share a glass of sweet tea or a bowl of Grandpa's homemade ice cream. To string beans and swap stories and to enjoy the peaceful scene of cows grazing in the pasture across from their house.

I wish I'd known then how precious those moments were. I do now, and I'm reminded of how all the moments we've lived through become the fabric of our lives, the plan carefully stitched together by the One who designed us.

If we've lived for Him, our testimonies are—like Granny's quilts—a patchwork of memories. Of moments when we've experienced His faithfulness. Of times we've had the privilege of working for Him. Of answered prayers. Of sweet times we've worshipped with His presence hovering close by. They're reminders of His blessings.

I'm so grateful for the moments when I've been wrapped in my grandmother's quilts. And even more for all the moments when I've been wrapped in God's love. There's not a warmer or more comforting feeling on the face of this earth.

Lord, just as I'm grateful to have my grand-mother's quilts, I'm so thankful that I have precious stories of the times You've comforted me. Remind me to tell others about the moments You've provided what I've needed. About the days when all hope was gone—and then You showed up. And about the nights You soothed my broken heart. Just as Granny's quilts have comforted and warmed my family, use my life to share Your comfort and love with others. Amen.

A LITTLE Gravy ON TOP

1. Quilts provide warmth on cold winter nights, and God's presence provides warmth during those winter seasons of our lives. Write about two instances where God has comforted you and then share those stories with your loved ones.

2. Quilts are often handed down from generation to generation. It's even more important to hand down our faith to the generations that will come after us. What are some steps you can take to do that?

3. Granny's quilts are a patchwork of memories from days gone by. What are some of your best faith-filled memories of loved ones?

4. What are specific character traits and faith elements that you want to hand down to your children and grandchildren?

5. Quilting bees were also times of fellowship. Spending time with other believers is important. It strengthens us and our faith. What can you do to spend time with and encourage your loved ones and other fellow believers?

Dried Apple Fried Pies

(From the kitchen of Granny Bessie Cox)

    1 cup self-rising flour
    ⅓ cup shortening
    milk
    (OR 1 large can flaky biscuits for updated recipe)
    dried apples (or fresh apples)
    ½ tablespoon lemon juice
    sugar
    cinnamon
    canola oil
    1 teaspoon butter

Original Recipe

Cook a bag of dried apples (with lemon juice) in a large microwave-safe bowl. Add enough water to almost cover the apples. Cover the bowl with wax paper. Cook on high power. Stir and continue cooking until the apples are tender. (Or cook fresh apples on the stove with lemon juice and enough water to cover them, until they are tender and slightly chunky.) Drain excess water. Add sugar and cinnamon to taste.

Stir the flour, shortening, and milk together. Add the milk slowly until the dough is workable and does not stick to hands. Pinch a small amount, make a ball, and roll out. Place the cooked apples in the dough, leaving the edges clean. Fold in half and then take a fork and seal the edges. Place in hot oil until golden brown. Flip over and brown on the other side.

Updated Recipe

Split each biscuit from a can of flaky biscuits in horizontal halves so each biscuit makes two equal circles of dough. Roll each piece on a floured surface until thin and round.

Place a spoonful of the warm sweetened apples (see original recipe above for instructions) in the center of each biscuit, keeping the edges clean. Fold the dough over and seal the edges with a fork. Heat the oil and butter over medium- high heat. Fry each pie until golden brown and then flip over and brown on the other side. Remove and place on paper towels. Enjoy while still warm.

Note

This would also be good with canned cherry or peach pie filling in place of the apples.

CHAPTER SIXTEEN:

Southern Characters

*But indeed for this purpose I have raised you up,
that I may show My power in you, and that My
name may be declared in all the earth.*
Exodus 9:16 (NKJV)

"Nobody else has our exact talents and life experience. God
gave them to us to use for Him—and if we don't use them,
our part in His plan will be left undone."

The South is known for having some real characters. My dad was one of them. I never knew what to expect from him, but I discovered that his actions either left me laughing or shaking my head in disbelief.

I once got a phone call from him. "I have great news. We've both won watches."

I said, "How did *we* win watches?"

"Well, a jewelry store had a contest where folks could nominate volunteers who were helping their communities in big ways, so I wrote a letter about me and signed your name on it. We won."

On another occasion, Dad had his turn signal on, waiting for a car to pull out of a parking space. The second the car exited the spot, a little sports car zipped in front of him and pulled into it. The young man got out and waved. "That was for you, Grandpa."

Dad drove off. When the young man went into the mall, Dad pulled up to where his parking space should have been. And then he let the air out of all four tires on the guy's car and left a note on the windshield: "That was for you, Grandson."

Yes, many of our conversations began with, "Daddy, I can't believe you did that." But I suspect that young man never pulled that number on a senior citizen again.

Several years later, I drove to Atlanta to visit for a few days. My aunt and uncle were there from Kentucky, and my aunt said, "Come outside and see if you know what kind of bush this is in your dad's landscaping."

We walked to the front yard and she pointed at a bush. I said, "I don't know what it is." And that's when she explained why it was an odd shade of green. It seems the bush had died and the leaves had turned brown. So Dad bought a spray can of green blackboard paint and, about every six weeks, sprayed the bush with it. Yes, my dad invented the *Blackboardus Evergreenus* bush.

Dad gave us lots of funny memories, but he also touched many lives. Using his athletic skills, he coached thousands of young people. He made countless pots of chili for church and charity fundraisers. He volunteered for numerous organizations.

Dad was truly unique. But God made each of us a one-of-a-kind creation. Nobody else has our exact talents and life experience. God gave them to us to use for Him—and if we don't use them, our part in His plan will be left undone.

Could God use your sense of humor to help you work with teens? Could you encourage a young mom, or could He use you as a speaker, writer, or prayer warrior?

How will *you* be remembered? It's great for folks to talk about our funny moments together, but what really matters is that we've touched lives for God and fulfilled the plan He has for us.

Lord, just as Michelle's dad was a unique character, You've made each of us as a one-of-a-kind creation. We know You have a purpose for us, and we want to be faithful to fulfill it for Your glory. Remind us that none of our life experiences go to waste, and that You can use them if we'll let You. Help us to use every scrap of the talents and gifts You've given to us. Amen.

A LITTLE Gravy ON TOP

1. Michelle's dad was a character. He was known for his funny antics, but he was also known for the ways he helped people. What kind of reputation do you have? At the end of your life, what will people say about you—and more importantly, what will God say about you?

2. The letter to the jewelry store (supposedly from Michelle) represented her dad's accomplishments. To those around us, we are representatives of God. Are we reflecting His power and declaring His name to others?

3. Michelle's dad covered up the dead leaves on his bush with green blackboard paint—but that didn't make the bush flourish. Are you covering up things in your life? What do you need to change? Do you need a fresh application of Jesus?

4. What gifts and talents has God given to you? Think through them individually. How could each one be used for Him?

5. What purpose do you think God has for you? What can you do to achieve that purpose and to declare His power throughout the land?

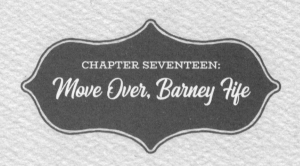

CHAPTER SEVENTEEN:

Move Over, Barney Fife

Behold, he who keeps Israel will neither
slumber nor sleep.
Psalm 121:4 (ESV)

"The great news is that while we sometimes are asleep on the job spiritually, God **never** slumbers. He's waiting right where we left Him, and all we have to do is make our way home to the security of a God who's **never** asleep on the job."

Just in case any of you have aspirations to become robbers, I thought it might be a good idea to tell you that planning the heist of a church in the South probably isn't a good idea. With security teams and all the armed good ol' boys in the congregations, you might find more firepower there than in many big city police departments. And unlike Barney Fife, they don't keep their bullets in their pockets.

So now that we have that out of the way, we can move on to something that happened at church one Wednesday night. We'd arrived a bit late, so we sat at the back. Soon after we took our seats, I heard an odd whirring noise, somewhat like a child's toy being wound. But the sound just kept going and going.

A bit later, my husband poked me with his elbow. He had a big grin on his face as he motioned toward the back row of the section beside us. That's when I discovered the source of the sound. A man from our church, George, was sitting on the back row, head tilted back, snoring like a chainsaw at a national chainsaw competition. There's no doubt in my mind that he would have won the prize.

The loud snoring continued through the opening songs. Through the sermon. Through the closing invitation. And even as folks were leaving after the service.

I figured I'd better wake George up. When I tapped him gently on the shoulder, he looked up at me with glassy eyes. I said, "George, church is over. You need to wake up so you can go home."

But I didn't discover the best detail of the story until later. It seems that snoring George had been our security detail for the service that evening. I had mental images of the robbers trying to wake him up. Yes, move over, Barney Fife—you've got competition now.

You know, friends, some of us are just like George. No, we didn't fall asleep in church (well, at least *this* time), but we've fallen asleep on the job spiritually. We didn't mean to, but we did. We let the busyness of life steal our times of Bible reading and prayer. We skipped church services because we were tired or had other things to do—and before we knew it, we were far away from God.

Does that sound familiar? When we find ourselves distanced from God, it's never because He's moved away from us. Friends, consider this your gentle tap on the shoulder. Your wake-up call. Away from God is a dangerous place to be, and it will affect your family as well as you.

The great news is that while we sometimes are asleep on the job spiritually, God *never* slumbers. He's waiting right where we left Him, and all we have to do is make our way home to the security of a God who's *never* asleep on the job.

Father, I want to be close to You. But, instead, I wander away. I fall asleep on the job spiritually. I allow other things to come into my life that separate me from You, and I become too busy for the God who loves me. Lord, help me get my priorities straight. Bring me home to You whenever I wander astray. I'm so grateful that You are never asleep on the job, that You're always waiting for me, and for the security that brings. Amen.

A LITTLE Gravy ON TOP

1. George fell asleep on the job. His error could have caused harm to others. When you fall asleep on the job spiritually, it can harm those you love. How can you avoid that situation?
2. Think of a time when you've felt distant from God. What circumstances brought that about? How did you feel when that happened?
3. Why is it dangerous to be distant from God?
4. What do you need to rearrange in your life so that you'll stay close to Jesus?
5. The Bible says that God never slumbers. What kind of security does that give you?

CHAPTER EIGHTEEN:

The Blessing of Biscuits

For it is God who is at work in you, both to will
and to work for His good pleasure.
Philippians 2:13 (NASB)

"Sometimes God makes us wait for things and we become impatient, wondering why He isn't answering our prayers—but just as a biscuit baker knows how long to handle the dough, He knows how to handle all the details of our lives."

A Southern mom planned a trip with some friends. They loaded their luggage in the car, drove down the driveway, and were almost out to the road for their fun weekend when the teenage daughter came racing across the yard frantically waving at them. "Wait! Wait!" They stopped the car, and when they rolled the window down, the teen said, "Momma, just in case something happens to you while you're gone, did you write the biscuit recipe down?"

Yes, folks, we take our biscuits seriously in the South. Whether topped with gravy, butter and jelly, honey, or with a piece of chicken or sausage tucked into the fluffy perfection, it's hard to find better eating. Well, unless one turns the dough into fried pies, sausage balls, or chicken and dumplings.

And, for the record, few self-respecting Southern women would *ever* use those whop-'em biscuits to serve with Sunday dinner. For those of you who ain't from around here, whop-'em biscuits are those canned biscuits in the dairy case—the ones where you whop the can on the counter and dough comes plopping out. Sweet mercy.

Sometimes it's the men in the family who bake the biscuits. My uncle was famous for the cat-head-sized ones he served with breakfast, and my son's biscuits are way better than the ones I make.

Many Southern kitchens have hosted scenes with one generation teaching the next the ins and outs of biscuit prep. And often, besides receiving the family biscuit recipe, a granddaughter or grandson is blessed to inherit their grandmother's rolling pin, measuring cup, or biscuit cutter.

A perfectly made biscuit is worthy of a moment of silence. And that's exactly what happens when the family gathers around the table and dives into the fluffy perfection. There's an art to making biscuits. The right ingredients. The right temperature. And just the right amount of time handling the dough.

Biscuit-making is a lot like our daily lives as Christians. God knows just what circumstances and challenges we need each day to make us become what He desires for us to be. Some days are easy, like a relaxing day on the porch swing with a soft breeze blowing. And then at other times, our spiritual journey can feel like we've been placed into the fire of affliction. Shucks, just ask Shadrach, Meshach, and Abednego. They can tell you all about that. But the good news is that God doesn't just leave us there. He knows exactly what we need.

Sometimes God makes us wait for things and we become impatient, wondering why He isn't answering our prayers—but just as a biscuit baker knows how long to handle the dough, He knows how to handle all the details of our lives. We just need to leave ourselves in His oh-so-capable hands instead of taking things into our own hands. Because nobody likes a crumbly or tough biscuit... or a crumbly or tough Christian.

*Lord, just as we make biscuits for our plea-
sure, I want my life to be a pleasure for You.
Make me pliable in your hands as You add the
ingredients I need in my life each day. When I
go through fiery trials, help me learn what You
want me to learn from those situations. I'm so
grateful You know exactly what I need for me
to become the person of faith that You desire for
me to be. Make me into something beautiful for
Your glory. Amen.*

A LITTLE Gravy ON TOP

1. One generation often passes down biscuit-making techniques to the next generation. Why is it important for you to pass down your faith in the same manner?
2. Families enjoy those light and fluffy biscuits their loved one makes. How can your life as a Christian also bring joy to others?
3. Biscuits need the right ingredients to turn out well. What ingredients do you need in your life as a Christian each day?
4. The biscuit dough must be baked at the right temperature. If the heat is too high, the biscuits will burn. God knows just when to apply the heat to our lives, but He never takes it too far. What did you learn from a situation where God turned the heat up in your life?
5. The biscuit dough must be handled just right or the biscuits will crumble or become tough. What could cause us to crumble or become tough spiritually?

Southern Buttermilk Biscuits

(From the kitchen of Michelle Cox)

Most great Southern cooks don't use a recipe for their biscuits. The technique is in their heads, the lessons passed down from previous generations. They know the dough is what they want when it passes the hand feel test as they work with it. Here's a basic recipe, but as you become experienced at making biscuit dough, you'll just add a dash of this and a dollop of that until it reaches perfection.

    2 cups self-rising flour
    3 tablespoons shortening
    ⅔ cup buttermilk
    Approximately 2–3 tablespoons butter

In a large mixing bowl, combine the self-rising flour and the shortening. Cut the shortening into the flour with a pastry blender. (Or use two table knives held side by side if you don't have a pastry blender.) Add the buttermilk until the mixture is a soft consistency.

Turn the mixture out onto a lightly floured surface. Sprinkle a little flour on top of the biscuit mixture. Flatten it with a rolling pin to about a half-inch thickness. Use a biscuit cutter (or a drinking glass if you don't have a biscuit cutter) and place the cut-out biscuits onto a baking plan. Put a small dab of butter on top of each biscuit. Bake for 15 minutes at 425° or until the biscuits are golden brown.

CHAPTER NINETEEN:

Second Chances

This I recall to my mind, Therefore I have hope.
The Lord's lovingkindnesses indeed never cease,
For His compassions never fail. They are new
every morning; Great is Your faithfulness.
Lamentations 3:21–23 (NASB)

"God gives us multiple chances to fix what we mess up in our lives. He knows we're often weak. He knows our faults and failures. He could give up on us and turn His back on us. Instead, He tells us that His mercies are new every morning."

S outhern men can fix anything. Well, at least they
think they can. Even if they've never done it before.
And even if they don't have a clue how to do it.

Just ask Laurie, a Southern wife whose dryer quit
working. As any mother with multiple children will tell
you, it's a big deal being without a washer or dryer. The
dirty clothes pile up quickly and become a mountain of
laundry. Laurie wanted to call a repairman. They had a
trusted one they'd used before. He usually responded
quickly, and she'd be back in the laundry business before
the day was over.

But this time, Laurie's husband, Al, and his buddy
Don were convinced that they could put the new belt on
the dryer without any problem. They pulled the dryer out
where they could work on it. Grunts, moments of silence,
and suggestions back and forth filled the laundry area
as they worked.

Laurie stayed out of the way, kind of enjoying the
Laurel and Hardy show going on down the hallway. As the

hours ticked by without any progress, she prayed they'd get her dryer fixed sometime before the month was up.

Laurie got busy working, and a few hours later she walked by their foyer again and stood there in shock. Her dryer was now literally in dozens and dozens of pieces. Screws, bolts, and parts covered the large foyer and over-flowed into the living room.

It took a while longer for the two guys to admit defeat. Laurie called the repairman. When he arrived at the front door, Laurie opened it wide and stepped out of the way so he could see her new dryer parts factory.

His jaw literally dropped, and without taking a step into the house, he slowly said, "I don't think I know how to fix that. If your husband and his friend can put it back together, I'll come fix the dryer belt." Laurie still giggles whenever she thinks of that moment.

To her amazement, Al and Don actually pieced it back together. Laurie called the repairman, and he came and installed a new dryer belt. And then he said, "If they ever try to do this again, they just have to remove this one piece to get to the belt."

Al and Don had a second chance to fix what they'd messed up. And you know what? God gives us multiple chances to fix what we mess up in our lives. He knows we're often weak. He knows our faults and failures. He could give up on us and turn His back on us. Instead, He tells us that His mercies are new every morning.

God's heart is touched by what touches us, and He will always be compassionate toward us. He gives us hope. His lovingkindness toward us will never end, and we can count on Him to be faithful to us—even when we've caused way bigger messes in our lives than Al and Don did while working on that dryer.

Lord, I mess up so often. I mean to do what's right, but I somehow end up doing just the opposite. I'm so grateful You're a God of mercy. You've proven that to me so many times. Forgive my failures and faults. Thank You that even when I mess up, You're still compassionate toward me, and that Your lovingkindness toward me will never end. You could give me what I deserve, but instead, You give me hope and love. Thank You so much, Lord. Amen.

A LITTLE Gravy ON TOP

1. Al and Don didn't know what to do, but they tried anyway. Sometimes we *do* know what to do, and yet we do just the opposite. Why do you think we act that way?

2. The two men had a second chance to try to put the dryer back together. God gives us multiple chances when we mess up—He just wants us to repent and come back to Him. Why do you think He does that?

3. Often, we wouldn't mess up at all if we'd seek guidance from God first. What are some occasions when you've done that in the past?

4. Sometimes our mess-ups leave scars on our lives and on the lives of others. How can you avoid that?

5. God's mercies to us are new every morning. Do you treat others with that same kind of mercy?

In everything set them an example by doing what is good. In your teaching show integrity, seriousness and soundness of speech that cannot be condemned, so that those who oppose you may be ashamed because they have nothing bad to say about us.
Titus 2:7–8 (NIV)

"Let's determine that we'll live each day as if Jesus was watching our every moment—because He is—and if He's pleased by what He sees, we won't ever have to worry about being a negative influence on others."

S arah and Mike live in the country, so they don't get many unexpected guests. Their loved ones always come in through the back door, so Sarah and Mike know that whenever someone arrives at their front door and rings the bell, it's somebody they don't know.

That happened a while back. Mike had arrived home from work. Sarah heard him go upstairs and then she heard the sound of water in the shower. She was starting dinner when the doorbell rang. She opened the front door and discovered three women from a religious group that often visited the community.

Now to understand the rest of the story, it's important for you to know the layout of Sarah and Mike's house. They have a large foyer. The women at the front door would have seen the stairs and the upstairs hallway at the top of the stairs. While talking to the women, Sarah's back would be to the stairs. Got it?

Sarah opened the front door wide, and she and the women had a nice conversation. She was a bit surprised when the women left in a rather abrupt manner, but she assumed they had other houses to visit.

A little later, Mike came downstairs, "Did I hear somebody ring the doorbell?" He got a funny look on his face when Sarah replied that he did and explained who was there. He said, "Did you talk with them? Were they here long?" Sarah replied that they'd talked a while, and then asked why he wanted to know, since Mike was acting odd.

"Well," he said, "I turned the water on in the shower and then I got busy upstairs for a little while. Then I went in the bathroom, got undressed for my shower, and realized I'd forgotten my clothes, so I walked down the hall to our bedroom and then walked back down the hall to the bathroom again."

Eyes big, Sarah gasped, "Did you have *any* clothes on?"

He shook his head. "Buck. Nekked."

He'd been completely oblivious upstairs. Sarah's back was to the stairs and the upstairs hallway, so she'd been totally unaware of the show going on behind her. But those poor women!

Sarah and Mike must be on a blacklist somewhere. After years of visits from this group, they haven't had another one since. Oh my.

You know what, though? It's not usually a dramatic moment like Mike had (for which we're all grateful), but the truth is that we never know who's watching us as we go about our lives each day. Our character shows through in the little moments.

And that's what can be scary when we think about it: are we leading people to God or are our actions turning people away from Him? Let's determine that we'll live each day as if Jesus was watching our every moment—because He is—and if He's pleased by what He sees, we won't ever have to worry about being a negative influence on others.

Father, I so often forget that others are watching me each day. I suspect they're often disappointed by what they see. I'm sorry, Lord. Help me to live like Jesus every day. Help others to see You in me and let my actions lead them to You. It would break my heart to know that my life turned people away from You, so teach me to be like You each day. Give me the character of Jesus in all that I do. Amen.

A LITTLE Gravy ON TOP

1. Mike had no idea that those women were at the door that day, and often we have no idea that others are watching us as we go about our daily lives. What kind of difference should that make in your Christian walk each day?

2. What does it mean when we say that our character shows through in the little moments, and how does that impact you?

3. How can your actions turn people to—or from—God? And what can you do about that?

4. Why does it make a difference to remember that Jesus is watching you each day?

5. You never know who is watching you. Have you ever had someone come to you and tell you that they've been watching your life? How did that make you feel?

CHAPTER TWENTY-ONE:
Jimmy Carter and Mother's Potato Salad

Above all, keep loving one another earnestly, since love covers a multitude of sins. Show hospitality to one another without grumbling.
1 Peter 4:8–9 (ESV)

"My mom used her culinary gifts to serve up heaping helpings of love piled high with sugary sweetness and a dollop of buttery goodness on top. Serving others was her legacy and her spiritual gift."

A buzz rippled across the pews. The pastor announced that the following Sunday, President and Mrs. Carter would attend the morning service, and would also join them for dinner on the grounds. My mother could hardly contain herself.

My father wasn't all that impressed. President Carter was a Democrat, he reminded Mother. But when it came to home cooking, Kathy Starnes was bipartisan. She believed that world peace could be achieved through a table piled with country fried steak, buttermilk biscuits, butter beans, sweet potato pie, and sweet tea.

Mom left church with a newfound purpose. She was determined to prepare a dish that would be a turning point in American politics. The dish she selected: potato salad. Mom ordered Dad to the supermarket with a list of ingredients. Only the finest would do—potatoes, onions, celery, mayonnaise, and her secret ingredient: a dash of mustard. She made countless practice batches, much to the chagrin of my father, who didn't care for potato salad.

By Thursday, mom was exasperated. The potato salad was either too lumpy or too mushy. She huffed out of the kitchen. "I've only got seven days to get this right."

My dad wasn't very helpful. "It only took God six days to make the world." Fortunately, she didn't have a cast iron skillet handy. But by Sunday morning, she produced a potato salad worthy of a peanut-farmer-turned-president.

There's nothing quite like dinner on the grounds. After the sermon, the congregation gathers in the fellowship hall, where tables are piled with fried chicken, country hams, Jell-O salads, biscuits, greens, and more pies than you can shake a stick at. Everything is made from scratch. Showing up at a Baptist church with a bucket of store-bought chicken just might get you kicked off the membership roll.

Mr. Jimmy and Miss Rosalynn began loading their plates, and both managed to find room for some of my mother's potato salad. A while later, Miss Rosalynn came over to meet my mom, and she pronounced the potato salad absolutely delicious.

It seemed like such an insignificant moment in life, but to my mother, that compliment from First Lady Rosalynn Carter meant the world. My mother found joy in cooking a good meal and found satisfaction in the full bellies and empty plates at her table.

At my mother's funeral many years later, I thought about that Sunday afternoon in the north Georgia mountains. The preacher asked for people to share something special about my mom. The piano player went first. She said it might seem odd, but she would always remember my mom's sweet potato pie. Then, somebody else mentioned her cornbread dressing. There were a few nods and amens. Aunt Lynn got teary-eyed when she talked about Momma's ambrosia.

And then I remembered my mother beaming with pride at her presidential potato salad.

She used her culinary gifts to serve up heaping helpings of love piled high with sugary sweetness and a dollop of buttery goodness on top. Serving others was her legacy and her spiritual gift.

Lord, I sometimes feel as if I have nothing to offer You or others. But then You remind me that You can use even tiny things for Your glory. You give all of us different abilities. Help me to use the spiritual gifts You've placed in me. And that includes preparing meals for others who are going through difficult times, for young moms who need a break from fixing dinner every once in a while, and for folks whose hearts will be touched by a plate of cookies or a sweet potato pie. Amen.

A LITTLE Gravy ON TOP

1. Kathy Starnes loved on others through the gift of her home-made treats. How can cooking show God's love to others?
2. What are your spiritual gifts? What are the skills and talents that God has placed in you?
3. How can you use those spiritual gifts for Him?
4. In our busy lives, hospitality often falls by the wayside—yet it can be a true gift to someone who is lonely or needs to feel loved. When's the last time you offered hospitality to someone who needed it?
5. Have you ever noticed that we don't forget people who are kind to us? Think of someone today who needs a batch of kindness and a heaping helping of God's love and reach out to them.

Sunday Potato Salad

(From the kitchen of Kathy Starnes)

10–12 medium potatoes, as uniformly sized as possible
8–10 hardboiled eggs
mayonnaise
1–2 tablespoons mustard
1–2 tablespoons Vidalia onion, diced
1–2 tablespoons sweet pickle relish or cubes
½ cup diced celery
salt and pepper to taste
green olives *(leave them out if Todd's coming for supper—Michelle seconds that)*

Wash the potatoes. Cover them in cold water in a large pot. Cook over high or medium-high heat and boil them until done (when a knife inserted in the middle of the potato goes in easily). Remove from the stovetop; pour off the boiling water. Cover with cold water until the potatoes have cooled. When cool, peel and dice them. Boil your eggs for about 15 minutes. When done, drain them, and let them sit in cold water until cool. Peel and chop finely. Add to the potatoes.

Stir in enough mayonnaise to make it creamy. Add the mustard a little at a time until you reach the desired flavor. Add the chopped onion, sweet pickle relish or cubes, and the diced celery. Add salt and pepper to taste. (And if you insist, add the olives.) Stir well, taste, and add whatever is needed. Chill overnight so the flavors blend.

CHAPTER TWENTY-TWO:
The Biggest Redneck of All

*And I will be a father to you, and you
shall be sons and daughters to me, says
the Lord Almighty.*
2 Corinthians 6:18 (ESV)

"You know what's amazing? God loves you just as you are. With all your faults. With all your failures. Just because you're you."

My family has lived in the South for generations. Pride isn't an admirable trait, but this is probably a good place to admit that while many of the rednecks I know are wonderful salt-of-the-earth folks, without even really thinking about it, I'd always somewhat prided myself that I wasn't a stereotypical redneck.

There was no broken-down sofa on my porch. No ancient vehicles on cinder blocks filled my lawn. No chickens and goats ran loose through the yard. I didn't wear a shirt with the sleeves ripped out, one with the sleeves rolled up to hold a pack of cigarettes, or one that was short enough to leave my belly out for an airing.

I didn't chew or spit tobacco. There was no pickup truck with a loud muffler and a gun rack sitting in my driveway. And I certainly never had a discarded toilet planter in the midst of my landscaping. Yes, folks, I was officially not a redneck.

But then I began researching my family tree. I found some interesting things there. There were stories of previous generations who lived during difficult times, trusted

Jesus, and made it through. I found old family recipes that said to put the pies on a metal bucket lid to bake them in the wood cookstove. There were stories of family members who started churches.

There were records of life, death, and challenges. There was even one story of several young family members many generations back who were alone when winter hit. The Indians took them in and let them live with them. I loved finding all these fascinating stories.

As I continued my research, I found something I'd never heard about before. I discovered that my maternal grandparents were first cousins. I was floored when I learned that. I guess it made it really easy for the two families when the first cousins eloped and got married, since everybody already knew everybody else. And that's when something life altering dawned on me, something that took my breath away.

Y'all, I'm my own cousin!

Is it possible to be any redneckier than that? Let's see, does that make my children my third or fourth cousins? Once removed or twice removed? Try figuring out the family relationships for that one.

Friends, we laugh about this, but there's one family relationship we'll never ever have to think about being messed up. God says that we're His children—with all the privileges and benefits that come with that. That's huge for many of us who've never felt like we truly belonged or who've felt like outsiders and outcasts.

Maybe your mom or dad rejected you. Perhaps your siblings were the favorites and you felt like, no matter what you did, you'd never measure up. You know what's amazing? God loves you just as you are. With all your faults and with all your failures. Just because you're you. This will be the one relationship you'll never have to wonder about—because the family tree will always show that *you* are His beloved child.

Father, I have a messed-up family, don't I? I suspect all of us do in one way or another. God, I'm so glad that You have a track record of using messed-up people. I'm grateful there's not a perfect person—other than You—found within the pages of the Bible. That gives me hope, because I sure do want You to use my life for Your purposes. So take all the broken pieces of my life, my failures, and my faults, and turn them into something that You can use for Your glory. Amen.

A LITTLE Gravy ON TOP

1. Who are some of the messed-up families in the Bible? What can you learn from them?
2. Other than God, there are no perfect people in the Bible. Why do you think God planned it that way?
3. It's time to get personal now. What are some family relationships that have hurt you in the past? Why do you think God allowed those moments, and what have you learned from them?
4. How can God use all the past hurts and broken places in your life for His glory?
5. Are there any family relationships that you need to mend? What are some prayers that you need to pray for your family?

CHAPTER TWENTY-THREE:
Southern Rivalries

Esau held a grudge against Jacob because of the blessing his father had given him.
Genesis 27:41 (NIV)

"Friends, family is precious. Treat each other well and let the only rivalries that exist between you occur when your two ball teams are up against each other. Any others aren't worth it."

Sports are a big deal in the South. As a child, I spent countless summer afternoons watching the Braves play in Atlanta. That was in the era where Hank Aaron was about to break Babe Ruth's homerun record, and there was great anticipation as we waited to see if *this* would be the day when it would happen.

Basketball games included the excitement of Pistol Pete Maravich working his magic as we were treated to a dazzling display of his ball-handling skills. Those were fun days and great memories, but I've found that the real sports rivalries below the Mason–Dixon Line come into play with college ball teams.

Just ask any Bama fans, folks clad in Tennessee orange, or rabid Carolina or Duke fans. It's serious business, folks—and that team rivalry certainly existed in my family. My dad was a big supporter of the University of Kentucky and the University of Louisville. My husband and sons joined me as loyal fans of the UNC Tarheels. And that's where the family competitiveness kicked in.

We lived several states apart, so we couldn't watch the games together. But whenever one of Dad's teams played the Tarheels, he certainly made his presence felt. Every time his team pulled ahead on the scoreboard, our phone would ring one time. And we knew it was Dad rubbing it in. We'd do the same to him when Carolina took the lead.

But things kicked up a notch one year. Dad scoffed, "You can forget a bowl game. The only place your team is going is to the toilet bowl." We pretended to ignore him. And then the season moved on to basketball. Of course, we didn't rub it in a bit when the Tarheels won the national championship that year. (Yeah, right.)

Dad had a longstanding visit planned for that next weekend—and that allowed us to concoct a little surprise for him. Upon his arrival, he discovered the guest room was filled with Carolina blue balloons, and I'd even found a new Carolina blue toilet bowl brush to hang on the door of his room. It was one of the few times I ever saw my dad stunned speechless. That was a fabulous family memory, one that we've laughed about and talked about many times through the years.

I love sharing those memories together, but what I love even more are the times when we share about God and what He's done in our lives—and there's no rivalry there.

Rivalries can tear families apart. They can sow discord. Rivalries go all the way back to Bible times. Cain was jealous when Abel's sacrifice was more pleasing to God—and he ended up killing his brother. By tricking his father, Jacob received the blessing that should have been his brother Esau's. Esau was bitter and held a grudge against Jacob.

Friends, family is precious. Treat each other well and let the only rivalries that exist between you occur when your two ball teams are up against each other. Any others aren't worth it.

Lord, why is it so easy to hurt those I love even when I don't mean to? I don't want there to be rivalries between me and my loved ones, but I'm often jealous or have emotions in my heart that shouldn't be there. I know that's not right. So please give me a heart that loves others more than I love myself. When others wrong me, help me to forgive—even when forgiveness isn't asked for. Remind me that family is a precious gift, one that's to be treasured and cared for. Amen.

A LITTLE
Gravy
ON TOP

1. Sports rivalries can be fun, but family rivalries can break hearts. What can you do to avoid those moments when a wedge is placed between you and a loved one?

2. How can rivalries, past hurts, and jealousy tear your family apart?

3. How did Cain's rivalry toward his brother impact his entire family?

4. Who does it hurt most when a family member has a grudge? And how do you think God feels about family rivalries?

5. Have you thought lately about what a precious gift your loved ones are in your life? Are rivalries truly worth losing those people and the everyday moments you share with them?

CHAPTER TWENTY-FOUR:
Southern Ingenuity

Then he took his staff in his hand and chose five
smooth stones from the brook and put them in
his shepherd's pouch. His sling was in his hand,
and he approached the Philistine.
1 Samuel 17:40 (ESV)

"A Christian whose Bible has been used so much that it's held together with duct tape is a person who won't have to worry about falling apart themselves because the truths and sweet promises that they've learned from those pages will hold them together no matter what comes their way."

Southerners are known for their ingenuity. Our methods might be a bit unorthodox, but we'll get the job done. Take Rae, for instance. During a blizzard, her neighborhood was snowed in for a week.

Everyone quickly became stir-crazy, so they decided they'd bring whatever food they had and gather at one of the houses that evening. Nobody had anything sweet left, so Rae tried to think of something she could fix without electricity. Then she had a eureka moment: she could make fudge on the grill. She grabbed her trusty iron skillet, bundled up, and made her first batch of grilled fudge. It was slightly smoky, but a huge hit with folks who hadn't had dessert in days.

That wasn't Rae's only ingenuous culinary moment. She'd planned to make chocolate-dipped Rice Krispie Treats for a friend—and then it dawned on her that her microwave was on the blink, and she couldn't melt the dipping chocolate on the stove without it clumping. So she covered the heating pad with foil, placed a casserole dish with the chocolate on top of the heating pad, and covered the dish with foil. It took a while to melt, but it worked perfectly.

But the best creative moments for Southerners happen with a roll of duct tape. Why, we could probably fix the world with a couple of rolls. Just ask the people who've used it to capture flies or to hold loose wheelchair controllers in place. Some folks have used it to remove zits, to repair busted pipes, to fix torn hems or (ahem) for emergency repairs when they split their britches. Funeral home staff have even been known to use duct tape under clothing to keep necklines from gaping when they dress the bodies.

And one resourceful Tennessee woman even used duct tape to fasten her beautiful Bradford pear tree back together when lightning split it down the middle. The repair lasted for four years.

That's the thing about duct tape. It's a temporary fix. Kind of like what many of us use when we put a patch over our problems instead of facing them. A young shepherd boy named David faced a giant of a problem named Goliath. Instead of wearing armor and using the king's spear, David used some ingenuity and picked up five smooth stones from the stream. With God on his side, the Goliath-sized problem was permanently fixed.

That's where we'll always find the best solutions for whatever situations we face: from God and from His Word.

Some of us have been blessed to receive the Bibles that belonged to our grandparents. The pages are worn and falling apart from so much use. And many of the covers are duct taped together. A Christian whose Bible has been used so much that it's held together with duct tape is a person who won't have to worry about falling apart themselves because the truths and sweet promises that they've learned from those pages will hold them together no matter what comes their way.

Father, I so often face problems, and instead of turning to You, I try to fix things myself. Sometimes that puts a temporary patch on things, but often I end up making a bigger mess than what I faced in the beginning. A mess that You have to clean up for me. Remind me that You are the One who has the answer for any circumstance I encounter, and remind me to come to You first because Your solutions are always better than mine. Amen.

A LITTLE Gravy ON TOP

1. Sometimes it's easier not to face our problems, so we ignore them or apply a temporary fix that's the equivalent of duct tape. What situation do you need to ask God to help you fix?

2. Why do you try to solve your problems instead of going to God first for help?

3. How can your Bible be a source for answers to the circumstances that you face?

4. Why was David able to defeat Goliath when others could not?

5. Think of someone you know whose Bible is falling apart from being used so often. What can you learn from them?

Todd's Homemade "Mater" Sandwiches

(From the kitchen of Todd Starnes)

> vine-ripened Mississippi red tomatoes
> white bread (this is no time to go healthy)
> Hellmann's, Duke's, or Blue Plate mayonnaise
> salt
> cracked pepper
> napkins

Cut the tomatoes into thick slabs and liberally season both sides with salt and cracked pepper. (This is not the time to be conservative.)

Slather both slices of the bread with mayonnaise and gently place the tomatoes on the bread.

Now, if you are from Charleston or Savannah, you will probably want to remove the crust, cut the sandwiches into squares, and place them on a doily on the family china that your great-great grandmother hid in the cellar from General Sherman.

But if you're from north Mississippi, you'll simply carry your sandwich over to the kitchen sink, hunch over, and try not to get any of the drippings on your Ole Miss T-shirt.

Doug Collins, my good friend and the congressman from Georgia, once explained the finesse needed to feast on an honest-to-goodness tomato sandwich.

"It's not a real mater sandwich unless you have to lean over the sink to eat it," he told me.

And if you're really looking to up your mater sandwich game, consider substituting the white bread with one of those delicious biscuits on page 118.

CHAPTER TWENTY-FIVE:

The Hand of God

*For all the law is fulfilled in one word, even in
this: "You shall love your neighbor as yourself."
Galatians 5:14 (NKJV)*

"What happened that day at the coffee shop was a beautiful visual of God's command to love our neighbors as we love ourselves. And it's a wonderful reminder that seeing the hand of God at work will change you and others forever."

Photos from the Crave Coffee Bar & Bistro in Arlington, Tennessee, take your breath away as you contemplate what might have been. The place was packed with teenagers drinking coffee and studying for exams when the unthinkable happened: a car plowed through the building.

The driver had suffered some sort of medical condition, blacked out, and lost control of the car. The vehicle smashed through a wall of glass, plowed through tables, and came to a stop inside the coffee bar.

There were as many as thirty young people inside the popular hangout spot, and first responders surely imagined they would be facing a mass casualty event. But it turns out that only four teenagers were hurt—and those injuries were just cuts, scrapes, and bruises.

Some would say the young people were lucky, but Lana Hickey, the owner of the coffee bar, knows divine intervention when she sees it. After watching the surveillance video of the crash, she has no doubt that what happened inside her coffee shop was nothing short of a miracle.

"You see absolutely nothing but God's hand moving these kids," she said. "Every child in there was moved maybe by an inch of being completely plowed over by this vehicle. It was unbelievable."

Mrs. Hickey is a Christian, and her faith flavors the atmosphere of the coffee bar. Local residents gather to hold Bible studies and there's always Christian music playing in the background. It's a place known for giving back to the community.

So maybe it wasn't that much of a surprise when several dozen folks showed up a few hours after the accident to help repair the damage. And there was a lot of damage. The SUV hadn't just gone through a window; it had gone all the way through the coffee shop.

Within a matter of hours, local construction crews had installed a new wall while volunteers swept away the broken glass. A professional cleaning crew offered their services, and a local sign guy hung a new banner letting folks know the coffee shop was open for business.

"It was the most unbelievable feeling that I've ever had," Mrs. Hickey said. "They all have a giving heart just like we do. It's very humbling. It's a little bit of a tear jerker. I cried a little bit."

Neighbor helping neighbor was a beautiful sight, but that's what folks do in the mid-South. Pictures show a building filled with men armed with brooms sweeping up the debris, others cheerfully working on ladders as they repair damage, and still others building a wooden wall to cover where the car plowed into the building.

What happened that day at the coffee bar was a beautiful visual of God's command to love our neighbors as we love ourselves. And it's a wonderful reminder that seeing the hand of God at work will change you and others forever.

Do you need to love your neighbor as yourself today? One thing's for sure: both of you will end up being blessed.

Lord, it's an awesome thing to see the hand of God at work. Sometimes, we forget that You still work miracles today. Remind us of that, Father. Whenever we see a neighbor who's in need of assistance, help us to remember Your command to love others as we love ourselves. I thank You for the opportunities that I've had to do that in the past, because somehow when I set out to be a blessing to my neighbors, I end up being the one who is truly blessed. Amen.

A LITTLE Gravy ON TOP

1. It was so clear that it was the hand of God that protected the customers who were in the coffee bar that day. How can God get glory from moments like that?
2. What miraculous moments have you experienced in your life?
3. How can neighbor helping neighbor be an act of service to God?
4. What sometimes keeps you from loving others as yourself?
5. How can it end up being a blessing to you when you set out to help a neighbor or other person who needs assistance? How can that impact others for God?

CHAPTER TWENTY-SIX:

*A Funny Thing Happened...
at Church?*

*Not giving up meeting together, as some are
in the habit of doing, but encouraging one
another—and all the more as you see the
Day approaching.*
Hebrews 10:25 (NIV)

"Assemble at church. Laugh. Make sweet memories with
your family as you learn about God. I can promise those are
moments that you'll never regret."

Have you ever gotten tickled at church? It happens to the best of us. For example, near the end of the evening service at my church, a young boy had evidently misbehaved enough that he'd stepped on his mama's last good nerve. As she carried her son out the door, he yelled, "Y'all, pray for me!" The congregation lost it.

Our church had a time for prayer requests during the evening service. A sweet older lady stood and requested prayer for Jessie on *General Hospital* because she was having surgery the next day. Not long after that, the same lady requested prayer for her granddaughter. She said, "We had to take her to the doctor the other day, and the doctor said she had a raisin stuck up her nose. He said it must have been there a while because it stunk." I don't know how the pastor kept a straight face on that one, because everyone else was bent double laughing.

Another church across town had a poor man's supper prior to the service. For those of y'all not from the South, that's cornbread, chowchow (a type of relish), onions, and dried beans (*lots* of beans) often cooked with a ham bone.

A missionary from Israel was visiting at the church that night. Following the dinner, everyone moved to the auditorium, and after the preliminaries, the pastor asked the missionary to stand and blow the Shofar horn (made from a ram's horn) to show the congregation how it sounds. Well, let's just say he blew more than the Shofar horn. Needless to say, they were pretty much done at that point.

A pastor serving in the Arctic mission field was in the pulpit one day. He was preaching hard and God was moving when suddenly in the quietness, a cell phone started ringing. It belonged to an older lady who was sitting on the second row with her adult niece. The elderly lady was a bit heavyset and wasn't able to lean over easily to retrieve the phone from her purse on the floor. It kept ringing and ringing, and she kept hitting her niece telling her to grab the purse and turn it off—but the ringtone chorus of Johnny Cash's song "Ring of Fire" kept playing. The pastor closed his Bible at that point, and they attempted to sing the closing hymn through their laughter.

The Bible says not to neglect the assembling of ourselves together, and there's a reason for that. Church is a place where we learn the truths and precious promises from God's Word, where our children spend hours in Sunday school and in programs like Awana learning about Jesus and others who are mentioned in the Bible. It's a place where we can bond with fellow believers, encourage each other in the faith, support each other through difficult times, grow spiritually…and sometimes laugh.

Assemble at church. Make sweet memories with your family as you learn about God. I can promise those are moments that you'll never regret.

Lord, I thank You for the blessing of church. For a pastor who preaches about You. For friends who encourage me—and whom I can encourage. I'm grateful for what I learn there, for the messages that feed my soul and convict me as needed. I realize that church is the superglue to hold my family together. Thank You for all the moments—serious, poignant, and funny—that are part of my memories from church. Help me to be faithful in my attendance. Amen.

A LITTLE
Gravy
ON TOP

1. Why do you think God tells us not to neglect the assembling of ourselves together at church?
2. What are some of the blessings you gain from faithful attendance at church?
3. What are some of your best memories from church? Serious ones? Poignant ones? Funny ones?
4. How does attending church together as a family serve as a superglue to bond your family together?
5. Are you faithful in your attendance, or do you need to make some changes? If so, what steps do you need to take?

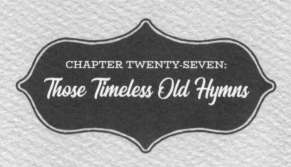

CHAPTER TWENTY-SEVEN:

Those Timeless Old Hymns

After consulting the people, Jehoshaphat ap-
pointed men to sing to the Lord and to praise
him for the splendor of his holiness as they
went out at the head of the army. As they
began to sing and praise, the Lord set ambush-
es against the men of Ammon and Moab and
Mount Seir who were invading Judah, and
they were defeated.
2 Chronicles 20:21–22 (NIV)

"When we sing, it moves our eyes from our circumstances
and brings our focus back to the God who is the answer for
all that we need."

I'd taken my sons to visit the grave of their great-great-great-grandmother. She'd been widowed and left to raise six children alone when her husband died in the Civil War. He wrote her a letter before he died and told her to raise the children for the Lord. She was faithful to do that, and she had donated the land for the church and cemetery where we stood—a church that was still thriving six generations later.

The day we were there, the melodious sound of "Jesus Loves Me" drifted down the hillside, sung by the children inside the church at vacation Bible school. It was a sweet reminder of the spiritual heritage with which many of us in the South have been blessed.

Hymns are a big part of that heritage. Many of us have poignant memories of moments with the old hymns. There were homecoming meals at church and singings on the grounds. Southern gospel groups sang to the accompaniment of banjos, mandolins, dulcimers, and other mountain instruments.

The old hymns are timeless. They have depth, and they prepare the heart for worship. And those familiar words have softened the hearts of numerous prodigals, bringing them back to God.

For many of us, those hymns have helped us make it through dark nights of heartache or despair. Many years ago, following a car wreck, I spent six weeks in the hospital. I was discouraged, in pain, and wondering if I'd ever walk normally again. I desperately wanted to be home with my husband and little boys.

I hit bottom one night, and I cried alone in the darkness of my hospital room. But then God sent the words of that beautiful old hymn, "'Tis So Sweet to Trust in Jesus" to my heart. The tears of despair changed to tears of thanksgiving as I softly sang that night, the words I'd learned as a child speaking comfort to my soul.

God often used music in powerful ways in His Word. There was an instance when the children of Israel faced a huge battle that terrified them. But as they began to sing, God fought the battle for them.

And think of Paul and Silas sitting in a dank prison cell. They'd been brutally beaten, thrust into the inner part of the jail, and shackled. The men must have been in pain, but around midnight, they prayed, and then they did something that must have sounded so alien in that prison:

they sang praises to God. Songs that must have touched the hardened hearts of the other prisoners.

Friends, are you in a dark place of despair right now? Are there situations that overwhelm you, circumstances where you see no way out? Start singing some of the old hymns. Let the words seep into your soul. I think you'll discover what I did in that lonely hospital room: when we sing, it moves our eyes from our circumstances and brings our focus back to the God who is the answer for all that we need.

Lord, thank You for those who've written the old hymns. Words that have been learned by experience and shared for others who would walk those same paths. I'm grateful for Your gift of music. There's something about singing or listening to folks sing praises to You that touches my heart, speaks to my soul, gives me hope, and has even provided conviction when needed. Help me to sing Your praises so that others can hear about my amazing God. Give me a song in the night—and help it to impact the lives of others. Amen.

A LITTLE Gravy ON TOP

1. Why are the old hymns still important today?
2. Have you ever had the words of a hymn you learned many years ago come to your mind just as you needed hope or encouragement? How did that affect you?
3. Why is it important for you to teach your children the words of those songs and other ones that give praise to God?
4. Paul and Silas sang in prison. What lessons can you learn from their response to difficult circumstances?
5. Why do you think the victory for the battle began when the children of Israel began singing and praising God?

Mama's Deviled Eggs

(From the kitchen of Michelle Cox)

I doubt that there's ever been a church homecoming dinner without trays of deviled eggs spread out on the buffet tables. They're a classic at most get-togethers like that.

Southern cooks are notorious for not measuring ingredients. We just add and sample until it tastes right, so these are the basics for making traditional Southern deviled eggs.

> large eggs
> mayonnaise
> salt
> mustard (plain yellow)
> paprika, optional

Boil the eggs for 15 minutes. Stir gently several times while boiling to help keep the egg yolks centered. At the end of the boiling time, remove the pot from the burner and drain off the hot water. Keep adding cold water until the water in the pot is good and cold. Let the eggs cool and then remove the shells. (It's much more difficult to shell really fresh eggs, so try to buy them at least a week or so ahead of when you're going to use them.)

Cut the eggs in half lengthwise. Remove the yolks and mash them with a fork until they're well mashed. Add the mayonnaise, salt, and a little mustard, tasting as you go to see what else is needed. Add more mayonnaise, salt, and mustard as needed until the deviled egg mixture is creamy and flavorful. Pipe or spoon into the egg white halves. Sprinkle with paprika if desired. Chill, serve on a pretty platter, and enjoy.

CHAPTER TWENTY-EIGHT:
A Miracle at Thirty Thousand Feet

*And my God will supply all your needs accord-
ing to His riches in glory in Christ Jesus.
Philippians 4:19 (NASB)*

"It was a reminder to me that God cares about every detail
of our lives. And all of us on board that Delta jetliner were
reminded that we serve a God who meets all of our needs—
even at thirty thousand feet."

Southerners are always willing to provide a helping hand whenever needed. It's what we do. If an elderly neighbor's sidewalk is covered with snow, we make sure it's clear. If someone's sick, we take them dinner and a vase of colorful flowers. And if someone's in need, we dip into our wallets and help to solve their problems, usually anonymously to save their pride.

But sometimes the call to action is for a much more important task than normal. I learned that a while back when I was on a flight to New York City. I noticed the flight attendants seemed rather preoccupied that day. They were rushing up and down the aisle.

An announcement was soon made that they needed a doctor. A passenger was in medical distress: she was having a heart attack at thirty thousand feet.

The passenger received an unexpected blessing that day, because it turned out there wasn't just one doctor on board: there were five—including a cardiologist. They worked to help the patient, but the doctors needed a way to monitor her vital signs, and this certainly wasn't the usual hospital setting with full equipment at their disposal.

But it just so happened that there was a gentleman on board with an app on his iPhone that provided the necessary data. Just what the doctors needed to help them as they tried to save the passenger's life.

A little while later, the public address system crackled to life with another request—they needed an unusual heart medication. And that's where I became part of this life-or-death drama in the sky.

Normally, I pack my heart medications in my checked baggage. But I had been running late for the flight, so I just stuffed the meds in my carry-on bag. And it just so happened that I had the heart medication the doctors needed. The exact unusual medicine.

The plane was diverted to Baltimore and the ailing passenger was able to be treated by paramedics. Less than an hour later, we were back en route to New York City.

A lot of people might have explained the day's happenings as a lucky coincidence. But I knew better. I knew beyond a doubt that every detail of that passenger's day had been planned by an almighty God who loved her. That nothing had just happened by chance.

It's not often that we get to have front row seats for a miracle, but that day we did. Not just one doctor on board, but five—and one of those just exactly what the passenger required. Another passenger who had an app that did just exactly what those doctors needed. And me. A heart surgery survivor whose medications were just exactly what the woman needed that day.

It was a reminder to me that God cares about every detail of our lives. And all of us on board that Delta jetliner were reminded that we serve a God who meets all of our needs—even at thirty thousand feet.

Father, sometimes when I'm in the midst of troubles, I forget that You have planned every tiny detail of my life. I should be able to look at the past and see where time and time again, You've been faithful, where You've supplied all that I needed. Sometimes I forget that You didn't quit working miracles just because the pages of the Bible ended. Help me to trust You more. What a blessing to know that You can meet all of my needs. Amen.

A LITTLE Gravy ON TOP

1. Do you think that all the things the passenger on that flight needed for her medical emergency just happened to be there? Why or why not?

2. Sometimes God places us at just the right place and time to be a blessing to someone or to help them. What are some times when that has happened to you?

3. God says that He will supply all your needs according to **His** riches. What difference does that make?

4. Why is it that when you face difficult circumstances, you so often forget how God has provided for you in the past?

5. What are three things you need to trust God with today?

CHAPTER TWENTY-NINE:
Watch Out for the Bears

Finally, be strong in the Lord and in his mighty power. Put on the full armor of God, so that you can take your stand against the devil's schemes.
Ephesians 6:10–11 (NIV)

"Friends, God's prepared a flyer for us in Ephesians 6:10–20. A life flyer that tells us how to be strong using the mighty power of God, and how to protect ourselves against the ploys of the devil."

Todd and I have been on faculty at the Blue Ridge Mountains Christian Writers Conference for many years. Nestled in the Black Mountain area of North Carolina, the campus is tucked into the side of a mountain and surrounded by wooded areas. It's a wonderful conference, and we've been there so many years that it feels like a family reunion when we're reunited each May with the wonderful faculty and folks who attend year after year.

But there's one memory that makes us laugh every time we think about it. During one of our first years at the conference, as we registered for the week in the large entry building, we noticed a yellow flyer sitting on the counter. Yes, folks, the infamous yellow bear flyer.

That flyer especially caught the attention of first-time attendees each year, and we often heard the question, "Are there really bears in the area?" The answer was yes. Bears were frequently seen on the grounds of the conference center.

The bear flyer contained instructions on what attendees should do in case they encountered any of the bears that lived in the mountains surrounding the campus. One of the most important items was that folks should never come between a mother bear and her cubs. Good advice.

And then it continued—never run when you encounter a bear. Back up slowly. Now I'm just going to tell you, that's probably not going to happen. If I'm standing there facing a big bear, I'm probably going to run before I even think about it.

Another piece of advice was to make a lot of noise and make yourself look as large as possible. I've nailed that one.

After years of experience, I've added a few things to my bear flyer list. It's probably not a good idea to be walking along with yummy-smelling food in your possession. You don't want to give the bear an idea for an all-you-can-eat-buffet—with you being the featured item on the menu.

And then there's my most brilliant idea. Forget the bear spray. Next time I'm on campus, I'm going to give honey-scented lotion to fellow attendees, and then I'll look for someone who runs slower than I do. Problem solved. Whew.

Friends, God's also prepared a flyer for us in Ephesians 6:10–20. A life flyer that tells us how to be strong using the mighty power of God, and how to protect ourselves against the ploys of the devil. God even gives us armor to wear—a breastplate of righteousness, the Gospel of peace to arm our feet, a shield of faith, and a helmet of salvation.

And then He gave us a powerful sword—His Word. All the instructions that we'll ever need are included there. If we follow God's life flyer for us, we will be able to stand strong and to open our mouths boldly to share the gospel—and that's far more important than the instructions on that bear flyer will ever be.

Lord, I realize that spiritual warfare is real and that the devil works hard to defeat us. I need Your armor and Your mighty strength to make it through each day. Thank You for our powerful sword—Your Word—and for the daily instruction I find there. Help me to stand strong for You and give me an amazing boldness so that I'll share the Gospel freely with those who so desperately need to hear it. Thank You for being my protector and my strength. Amen.

A LITTLE Gravy ON TOP

1. Why does the devil seek to defeat us in our daily walk as Christians? What are some of the ways that He does that?
2. Why is it important for you to put on the armor that God's given you?
3. What is the answer to defeating spiritual warfare?
4. Why does God call His Word a sword?
5. When you learn to be strong in Christ, He gives you boldness to open your mouth to share the Gospel with others. Who in your life needs to hear the glorious story of Jesus and His love?

CHAPTER THIRTY:
Southern Funerals

Because of the tender mercy of our God,
whereby the sunrise shall visit us from on high
to give light to those who sit in darkness and
in the shadow of death, to guide our feet into
the way of peace.
Luke 1:78–79 (ESV)

"Perhaps you're going through a time of loss that's broken your heart. The God who loves you so much that He gave His Son's life for you will never leave you alone, and He will not leave you comfortless."

Drive often enough through the South and sooner or later you'll see long lines of vehicles pulled over on both sides of the road. No, they haven't all developed car trouble. It's a gesture of respect for a funeral procession, for the family who has lost a loved one.

Church members and neighbors show up with casseroles and heaping platters of food, hugs that squeeze straight to your heart, and prayers that provide strength for the hard days ahead.

But sometimes, well, sometimes Southern funerals can get a little interesting. Reverend Johnson was asked to preach a funeral for a lady he'd never met. He talked to her family before the funeral, so he'd learn some personal things about her. He conducted a beautiful service as he told what a wonderful cook Ms. Ethel had been, about Ms. Ethel's sense of humor, how Ms. Ethel had loved her family, and how Ms. Ethel had been a faithful church member. There was just one not-so-slight problem: her name wasn't Ethel. Oops.

Years ago, families often had the body lie in state in their home. On one occasion, the staff at the funeral home went to a house and picked up the body, took it to the funeral home, groomed the body and dressed it, and took it back to the home so family and friends could pay their respects.

Several hours later, the staff went back to the house to return the body to the funeral home. When they got there, they were taken aback by the disheveled state of the body, and even more so when they discovered there was dirt on the deceased's clothes. "How did he get so dirty?"

A family member replied, "Oh, that must have happened when we stood the body up in the yard to take some family pictures."

Folks, you can't make this stuff up. The stories are funny, but the truth is that death will visit all of our homes at one time or another. It's an important reminder that each of us needs to be ready to meet God. If you haven't asked Jesus to forgive your sins and come into your heart, today would be the perfect day to do that.

For loved ones who are left behind, these are often dark times when we see no way out, when it doesn't seem like we'll ever smile again, when it doesn't seem the sun will ever shine again. But that's where the tender mercy of God will shine into our lives, lighting the darkness with His unexplainable peace.

These are the moments when we'll feel His comfort in a way we never have before, when we'll feel His arms wrap around us in love. Perhaps you're going through a time of loss that's broken your heart. The God who loves you so much that He gave His Son's life for you will never leave you alone, and He will not leave you comfortless. He's going to be enough for all the days ahead. You can count on it.

Father, I'm struggling with the loss of my loved one. This is a club I never wanted to join, but I had no choice in the matter. My heart is broken, and I'm having trouble functioning. I don't know how I'm going to go on without this one I loved so much, but You promise that You will never leave me comfortless. Lord, I'm so grateful that I don't have to go through this without You. Thank You for the peace You promise to give me. Amen.

A LITTLE Gravy ON TOP

1. Reverend Johnson used the wrong name during the funeral service, but God always knows your name. He knows your heart, and He knows when you are hurting. If it touches you, it touches Him. How does it make you feel to know that God hurts when you hurt?

2. It's not something we like to think about, but death will come to all of us. We have no guarantee of tomorrow. Do you **know** where you'll spend eternity? Would you like to ask Jesus to be your Savior today?

3. Have you experienced the loss of a loved one? What verse brought you hope or comforted you during that time?

4. God promises to give you light in the dark times of your life. What are some circumstances where God has done that for you?

5. How can your testimony of God's faithfulness be a blessing to someone else? Is there someone you can bring love and comfort to today?

Velma Haley's "Funeral Pie"

(Shared by Sarah Cannon)

My dear friend (and fellow Memphian) Sarah Cannon's aunt Velma Haley was notorious for keeping "funeral pies" in her freezer. So what in the name of Paula Deen is a funeral pie?

Well, it's this recipe for Velma's pecan pie. The pies freeze well, so she always kept some on hand in the freezer to take to the after party when there was a funeral.

But that wasn't Velma's only use for this pie. When neighbors had a party and Velma wasn't invited, she had her plan ready. Imagine the scene: cars are parked up and down the street in the neighborhood, and it's evident that the Smiths are having a party—one to which Velma didn't receive an invitation.

So, Aunt Velma would whip out a funeral pie from the freezer, go to the neighbor's house, and ring the doorbell. When Mrs. Smith came to the door, Velma would say, "I saw all the cars and thought someone must have died, so I made you this pie." And all of a sudden, Velma would receive an immediate invitation to the party.

3 eggs, beaten
½ cup of sugar
1 cup of dark Karo syrup
5–6 tablespoons of margarine or butter (approximately ¾ stick)
1 teaspoon of vanilla extract

1–2 cups of pecan halves (or chopped pecans if preferred)

1 unbaked pie shell

Preheat the oven to 350°. In a large mixing bowl, beat the eggs, and then add the sugar, Karo syrup, butter, and vanilla. Stir together and then add the pecans. Pour the mixture into the unbaked pie shell. Place the pie on a cookie sheet covered with foil in case the filling runs over while baking. Put in the preheated oven and bake for 30–45 minutes or until brown.

CHAPTER THIRTY-ONE:
*Love Hidden
in a Hurricane*

*Be devoted to one another in brotherly love; give
preference to one another in honor;
Romans 12:10 (NASB)*

"'Don't see guilt when you look out there—just see a back-yard where every surface has been touched by love.' And then I whispered, 'God, thank You so much for the precious gift of family.'"

Hurricanes often batter Southern states. But when Hurricane Michael hit the panhandle of Florida, it became personal. Our son's family lives there. Weathercasters initially expected minimal impact. The forecast quickly changed to a massive hurricane with a mandatory evacuation. Tim's family packed and headed a safe distance away.

We watched our television in disbelief as the monster hurricane pounded their town. Tim's family wouldn't be going home anytime soon. They arrived at our house the next day, battle-worn and weary, not knowing if they still had a home or job. Waiting for news was agony.

That's when love stepped in. Our other sons and their families showed up with dinner and hugs soon after Tim's family arrived. Our daughters-in-law brought bags filled with the warmer clothes they would need. I wiped tears away as Tim's brothers discreetly slipped him money. Friends and our church responded with cash and gift cards. The outpouring of love was so touching.

News reports showed Tim's area was one of the hardest-hit locations. A week later, a friend hiked in and took pictures. The massive old oaks now resided on the house, pool, and backyard. The damage was jaw-dropping, but their house was still standing. We all cried.

When residents were allowed back, my husband, sons, a friend, and my brother-in-law packed chainsaws, tools, food, and water and drove to Panama City.

They were greeted by ten members of my daughter-in-law's family who'd arrived early that morning to begin clearing a path. It makes me cry whenever I think of that scene, love in action as they all worked together in the extreme heat. They accomplished a lot in the time they were there, but with so much damage, there was still a mind-boggling amount left to do.

Several weeks later, our entire family took off work and headed to Florida. I'd seen pictures and videos, but seeing the carnage in person was shocking. Forty-plus days later, it still looked like a war zone. As we drove into Tim's neighborhood, we saw tarp-covered houses with towering piles of cut-up trees and debris lining the streets.

Fourteen of us set to work, family strong. Even the little ones helped. Fallen trees were cut up. The roof was replaced. We cleared up branches and other items, hauling countless wheelbarrow loads to the debris pile. The yard was like a busy beehive as we scurried about. Tears sprang to my eyes as I looked at the scene around me.

I saw the true beauty of family.

Loving hearts and helping hands accomplished a lot, and a few days later, the backyard was once again the beautiful place where our family has made memories. My daughter-in-law looked out her door that evening, "It makes me feel guilty that our place looks so nice when others don't."

I replied, "Don't see guilt when you look out there— just see a backyard where every surface has been touched by love." And then I whispered, "God, thank You so much for the precious gift of family."

Father, thank You for the gift of family. For loved ones to laugh with, to worship You with, and to go through life with, making memories. I thank You for the times my family has rallied together when difficult times arrived. It moves my heart to see the love in action. I'm so grateful that You loaned me my children. Each stage of their lives has been such a joy. Continue to bind our hearts together. Help us to love You and each other more and more as the years go by. Amen.

A LITTLE
Gravy
ON TOP

1. Why is your family such a precious gift from God? And when's the last time you stopped and thanked Him for your family members?
2. Why does loving each other make everyone feel good? And how does that please the heart of God?
3. Why does God sometimes give you unexpected blessings as you go through difficult times?
4. What are some ways that families can help each other through hard circumstances?
5. Love is the glue that binds families together. What can you learn about your relationship with your heavenly Father from your earthly family relationships?

CHAPTER THIRTY-TWO:
Southern Pranksters

*A merry heart does good, like medicine, But a
broken spirit dries the bones.
Proverbs 17:22 (NKJV)*

"Folks, laughter is a gift from God. Shared moments of
merriment bond us together with sweet memories. Laughter makes us feel better. It lightens our load during difficult
times. It changes the mood in our homes. And God says that
a merry heart is good for us—like medicine."

Southerners are notorious pranksters. It's never done to be mean. We only prank those we love. (Be sure to ask Todd about the snipe-hunting trip he took to North Georgia.)

My son, Jason, is a youth pastor. When he went to his first service at his church, his teens welcomed Jason by filling his vehicle with balloons. They didn't stop there.

The next morning, Jason opened his office door and discovered the teens had filled plastic cups with water. Every inch of the floor (other than where the door opened) was covered in cups.

In the years since then, he's opened his office door and discovered a jungle, with every plant and tree from the church décor residing in his office space. But there was one night when the prank might have run a little off the rails...

Jason and our oldest son, Jeremy, lived next door to each other at the time. Their houses were way out in the country. Both of them had long driveways. Jeremy's house was on the hill above Jason's, and one Saturday night around midnight, Jeremy called Jason and said, "Somebody pulled into your driveway, and they're just sitting there. I'm going to drive down and block them in.

He pulled behind the car, and Jason walked out onto his porch in his pajamas, holding a rifle by his side. Anybody messing around at that time of night had to be up to no good. But then a window rolled down and a quivering voice said, "Jason, it's us." Four of the teen girls from the church had decided to roll Jason's yard with toilet paper—only they're the ones who got the surprise that night.

The entire church laughed the next morning when Jason shared the story—and added how one of the girls had told her mom, "Then Pastor Jason came out with his rifle. And he was in his pajamas with deer heads all over them!" Yes, girls, that one backfired on you.

But the funniest prank happened when Jason started getting phone calls from people who were interested in his free llamas. He had call after call. One or two callers with foreign accents even mentioned that they wanted the llamas for a cookout. Jason didn't have a clue why they were calling him. So he asked the next caller, "Where did you get my phone number? I've never owned any llamas."

The man replied that there were posters all over town. There was a picture of llamas, information, and Jason's phone number on each one. Those jokesters win the prize for most creative prank.

Folks, laughter is a gift from God. Shared moments of merriment bond us together with sweet memories. Laughter makes us feel better. It lightens our load during difficult times. It changes the mood in our homes. And God says that a merry heart is good for us—like medicine.

Do you need a hefty dose of laughter today? God says it does our bodies good.

Father, laughter is such a wonderful gift. There are so many difficult moments in my life, and laughter makes such a big difference by lightening the burdens on my heart and easing the stress. Thank You for family and for sweet friends to do life with. Remind me to make spending time with them a priority. Help me to bring laughter and joy into the lives of others, especially those who desperately need it. Give me a merry heart so I can share the joy of Jesus. Amen.

A LITTLE *Gravy* **ON TOP**

1. God says that a merry heart, like medicine, does us good. Why do you think that is?

6. Laughter is a gift from God. How can laughter (or lack of laughter) change the mood in your home?

7. How can a merry heart make you feel better or lighten your load of stress?

8. Did you know that joy is contagious? How can you use a merry heart to share the joy of Jesus with others?

9. How can laughing together strengthen your bond with others and provide shared memories that you'll remember for a lifetime?

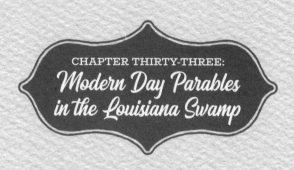

CHAPTER THIRTY-THREE:
Modern Day Parables in the Louisiana Swamp

*I shall walk before the Lord in the
land of the living.
Psalm 116:9 (NASB)*

"The Robertson family didn't hold back when it came to sharing their faith. Our world desperately needs Christians who'll boldly share about Jesus. And if more of us did that, our society would change."

I sure do miss *Duck Dynasty*. It really was a modern-day version of Mayberry—a television series that celebrated faith and family and ducks. It was back in 2012 that A&E introduced the nation to the owners of Duck Commander—my dear friends—the Robertson family of West Monroe, Louisiana.

It was only a matter of time before Phil and Miss Kay and Uncle Si and Willie became some of the most popular stars in reality television show history. Among all of us gun-toting, Bible-clinging deplorables, the Robertsons were beloved. Each week, they welcomed us into their homes and business for heaping helpings of fried frog legs, jugs of sweet tea, and a healthy dose of homespun humor.

On a side note, Willie Robertson gave me a *Duck Dynasty* Tupperware cup—just like the one Si had on the show. During a blizzard, I was dispatched to Central Park to deliver a live report during Megyn Kelly's primetime program. To illustrate just how cold it was in New York City, I filled the Tupperware cup with iced tea and set it on top of our satellite truck thirty minutes before my live television report. By the time I went on the air, the iced tea was frozen solid!

The Robertsons never shied away from their devout Christian beliefs, and I deeply respected that decision. One of the most poignant moments in each episode happened around the dinner table as the family held hands and prayed.

Phil is a regular guest on my radio show, and during one episode, he told me that beautiful moment of Christian fellowship was once considered controversial by the network's executives.

He confronted A&E after he realized they had been editing the name of Jesus Christ out of the family's supper table prayers. As it turned out, Hollywood did not share *Duck Dynasty*'s family values. Many of the popular magazines lashed out at the Robertson family's religious beliefs. One journalist called the Robertsons a "family of hypocritical Christian-right hillbillies."

"The show represented the pre-Trump Christian right's fantasy of itself—a family of hairy but God-fearing bootstrappers bowing their heads in prayer over the dinner table," the writer added.

It's no surprise that *Duck Dynasty* became the most watched nonfiction cable television show in history. American moms and dads had been clamoring for quite some time for family-friendly television programming—and Phil and Miss Kay and Uncle Si delivered the goods.

The Robertsons showed America that you can make it in show business without cursing, backstabbing people, or getting butt naked. Each episode was sort of like a modern-day parable, which wrapped up with the family gathered around the supper table, holding hands as somebody prayed.

I reckon that's why we loved *Duck Dynasty*; they made television family-friendly again. That's a fact, Jack (as Uncle Si might say).

The Robertson family didn't hold back when it came to sharing their faith. Our world desperately needs Christians who'll boldly share about Jesus. And if more of us did that, our society would change.

Lord, we thank You for the Robertson family of West Monroe. We thank You for their faithfulness and their Christian witness. Help us to be just as faithful to share about You with others. We thank You for sustaining them through the attacks of the evil ones. And we ask Your blessings on the entire family as they begin a new journey. May they be happy, happy, happy. In Jesus' name, amen.

A LITTLE Gravy ON TOP

1. The Robertson family stood out from other reality shows because they weren't ashamed to share their faith. How can you become bolder about sharing your faith?
2. Why is it so important for your family to gather around the table and pray together?
3. The Robertson family were role models for our nation. How could you be a role model in your home and community?
4. How can Christians living out their faith make a difference in our culture?
5. Do others know you're a Christian, or have you been keeping it a well-hidden secret?

Sausage Cheesy Grits

(From the kitchen of Orene McKenzie Blum,
Liberty Belles Literary Society)

Grits are a big part of our Southern culture and are often served at breakfast, as a savory side dish with bacon or sausage in them, or as an entrée with shrimp.

> 1 lb. hot sausage (or mild if you prefer)
> 4 cups water
> 1 cup uncooked quick grits
> 3 cups shredded sharp cheddar cheese, divided
> ¼ cup milk
> 2 tablespoons butter
> 2 teaspoons Worcestershire sauce
> 1½ teaspoons garlic salt
> 1 egg, beaten

Cook, drain, and crumble the sausage. Set aside. Cook the water and grits according to the package directions. Add two cups of the cheese and the milk, butter, Worcestershire sauce, and garlic salt. Stir until the cheese is melted. Combine a small amount of the grits mixture with the beaten egg. Add the remaining grits, stirring constantly.

Place half the grits mixture into an 8x8-inch baking dish that has been coated with cooking spray. Top with the crumbled sausage and then add the remaining grits mixture over the sausage. Cover the dish and refrigerate overnight.

See next Page...

Thirty minutes before you're ready to bake the cheesy grits, remove the dish from the refrigerator and let it stand at room temperature. Bake it uncovered at 350° for about 40 minutes. Add the remaining cup of cheese on top and bake for an additional 5 minutes. This will serve 8.

CHAPTER THIRTY-FOUR:
The Spice of Life

For everything there is a season, and a time for every matter under heaven: a time to be born, and a time to die.
Ecclesiastes 3:1–2 (ESV)

"There are many ways to have a long and healthy life, but there's only one way to have eternal life. And at the end of the day, that's all that matters."

Lois Wooten of Del City, Oklahoma turned 105 years old a while back. And as you might imagine, her birthday was mighty big news across the entire state.

Lawmakers invited Mrs. Wooten to the Oklahoma State Capitol, where she was given a special proclamation along with a heartfelt standing ovation. Let's be honest: it's not every day you get to meet someone who was born before the telephone was invented.

Mrs. Wooten grew up during the Roaring Twenties and learned how to drive behind the wheel of a Model T Ford. Mrs. Wooten decided it was time to hand over her car keys and her driver's license when she turned ninety-eight.

But even though she's not cruising around Del City, she still keeps up with modern technology. It turns out she has an iPhone, and she prefers keeping up with the family by texting.

Mrs. Wooten and her husband moved to the area in the 1950s. She managed the cafeteria at a local junior high school and her late husband was a firefighter at Tinker Air Force Base. They lived a very normal American life in a very normal American town. So how is it that Mrs. Wooten has lived to such an extraordinary age?

Television station KOCO dispatched one of their reporters to seek out the answer to the question that was on everyone's mind. Was it a healthy diet of fruits and vegetables? Did she refrain from drinking sweet tea and Coca-Cola? Was she a marathon runner and CrossFit trainer?

What in the name of Jack LaLanne was the secret to Mrs. Wooten's long and healthy life?

"I ate a lot of Kentucky Fried Chicken and Twinkies," Mrs. Wooten told the baffled news reporter. "I don't like to cook much. I eat a lot of frozen dinners. But who cares?"

Well, Sweet Methuselah! The magic elixir turned out to be a special blend of eleven herbs and spices—courtesy of Colonel Sanders. So the next time the doctor tells you to eat more arugula and less chicken fried steak, just tell him the story of Lois Wooten from Del City, Oklahoma.

We had a lot of fun with that story when I shared it on the radio program. And I was reminded of that beautiful verse from Proverbs 16:31 (GNT), "Long life is the reward of the righteous; gray hair is a glorious crown."

Discovering the fountain of youth has become a cottage industry across the fruited plain. It seems like every day there's some sort of fool-proof plan to live longer—from swearing off coffee to going vegan (not an option for most Southerners).

It's true: there are many ways to have a long and healthy life, but there's only one way to have eternal life. And at the end of the day, that's all that matters.

Father, You control the times and seasons of my life, and every breath that I take is a gift from You. Thank You for the assurance of eternal life. You paid the price with Your own life, and there are no words to thank You enough for loving me that much. Help me to share that news with others who need to hear it. When I come to the end of my days, help me to have lived in a manner where You'll be able to say, "Well done, good and faithful servant." Amen.

A LITTLE Gravy ON TOP

1. Lots of folks heard the story of Lois Wooten's life. What do you think people will hear about yours?

2. Proverbs 16:31 says, "Long life is the reward of the righteous." What do you think that means?

3. God's Word says there's only one way to eternal life, and that's through coming to Him, asking forgiveness for our wrongdoings, and inviting Jesus to come into our hearts. Have you done that? If not, today is the perfect time. If you have, when and where did it happen?

4. How does it make you feel to know that you will have eternal life—and to know the price that was paid for that?

5. Other people need to hear about the eternal life that is available to them and the hope that gives them. Make a list of three people you could talk to about God's love.

CHAPTER THIRTY-FIVE:
Pound Cakes and Sweet Faith

*Tell your children about it, Let your children
tell their children, And their children another generation.*
Joel 1:3 (NKJV)

There's no greater heri tage you can leave for your family
than the memory of a loved one who faithfully served God.

Pound cakes are a basic recipe for most Southern cooks. A slice fresh from the oven topped with juicy strawberries and whipped cream provides some mighty fine eating.

My earliest pound cake memories go back to when I was a little girl. My grandfather liked to cook, and he often let me help him. Family members still talk about his custard-based hand-churned ice cream, but my favorite moments in the kitchen with Grandpa were when he made his pound cakes.

I can close my eyes and still see the cloud of smoke as he turned the crank in the Hoosier cabinet and flour fell into the bowl. Perched on a chair, I watched him cream the butter and sugar together, and then I got to add the eggs, one at a time so Grandpa could whip the batter between each addition. Then we'd stir in the remaining ingredients until the mixture in the bowl reached perfection.

He'd pour the batter into a greased-and-floured pan and then we'd place it in the oven. And that's how I learned about Grandpa's baking secret.

Granny would sometimes say, "I wonder why your pound cakes always fall." Grandpa would turn and wink at me because the two of us knew the answer to that. You see, both of us liked the crunchy top on the pound cake, and Grandpa had discovered that if the cake fell while baking, there would be even more crunch.

So after the cake had baked for a little while, we'd slam the oven door a few times to make sure the cake fell, laughing together while we did it. I loved that Grandpa shared that little secret with me, and it's one of my favorite memories.

But there were other precious moments with Grandpa. That man loved God, and it was reflected in every moment of his life. He was a faithful member of the little white church that was next door to his house, and I have cherished memories of going with him early on Sunday mornings to unlock the building and ring the church bell so those beautiful clanging notes would echo throughout the community.

I don't ever remember Grandpa meeting a stranger without asking if he or she knew Jesus. He sent letters to his sons with advice on how they could become men of God. He wrote down his favorite Bible verses and shared them with his family.

He left me the legacy of his sweet faith, the example of how to love like Jesus, and the secret for crunchy pound cake crust. That's a mighty fine recipe for life.

And that leads to an important question: what spiritual legacy are *we* leaving behind for *our* families? That's something that all of us need to think about, and now is the perfect time to do it. Let's not look back with regrets and realize that we invested our time and talents in all the wrong things.

Dear Father, just as a pound cake emits a wonderful aroma while it bakes, let my life be a sweet fragrance of Your love. Thank You for the gift of those who've left our generation a spiritual heritage. Help me to be just as faithful, to love like You, and to leave behind a legacy of faith. When future generations look back at my life, help them to remember me as someone who loved and served You. Amen.

A LITTLE Gravy ON TOP

1. Michelle's grandfather took time to make memories with her. Life is busy these days. Are you making time to be with God and with those you love, or are you spending too much time on technology and other things?

2. Do you have family members who left you a spiritual heritage? What do you appreciate most about that, and how can you carry that faith to another generation?

3. Michelle's grandpa shared about his faith with everyone he met. When's the last time you told someone about God's amazing gift to us?

4. What will future generations say about you as a person? What will they remember about you and your faith? Do you need to make adjustments?

5. Have you shared your spiritual stories with your children and grandchildren? Have you told them about when you met Jesus? Have you shared your favorite Bible verses and why they are special to you?

Mother's Cream Cheese Pound Cake

(From the kitchen of Cindy Rushing, Liberty Belles Literary Society)

> 3 sticks unsalted butter, room temp
> 8 oz. full-fat cream cheese, room temp
> 2½ cups granulated sugar
> ⅓ cup sour cream, room temp
> 2 teaspoons pure vanilla extract
> 6 large eggs, room temp
> 3 cups cake flour
> ½ teaspoon baking powder
> ⅛ teaspoon salt

Preheat the oven to 325°. Coat a 10–12 cup Bundt pan with butter or nonstick cooking spray.

Beat the softened butter on high until creamy and smooth. This will take about 2 minutes. Make sure you scrape down the sides and bottom of the bowl several times throughout the mixing process so that everything blends well.

Add the cream cheese. Beat the mixture on high speed for about a minute, or until everything is blended and smooth, and then add the sugar, sour cream, and vanilla and beat the batter on high speed until everything is combined and creamy.

See next Page...

Add the eggs one at a time and beat on low speed. (Don't over-beat after the eggs have been added.) Once all the eggs have been incorporated, add the cake flour, baking powder, and salt. Beat on medium speed just until everything is combined. The batter will be creamy and thick.

Spoon the batter into the buttered or sprayed Bundt pan. Tapping the cake pan on the counter a few times will get rid of any air bubbles. Bake for 75–95 minutes. About halfway through, tent aluminum foil over the cake so that it doesn't get too brown. Use a toothpick or knife to test if it's done. If it comes out clean, it's done—but it does sometimes take the full 95 minutes.

Remove the cake from the oven. Cool it in the pan for two hours and then invert it onto a pretty serving plate. Allow to cool completely before covering it. This is awesome served with sweetened whipped cream and fresh berries. Enjoy!

Acknowledgments

A book like this involves many people, and we'd like to express our thanks to those who helped us bring *Our Daily Biscuit: Devotions with a Drawl* to fruition.

Thank you to all who shared their delightful Southern recipes, especially to Orene McKenzie Blum and the Liberty Belles Literary Society who sent us a file filled with wonderful recipes. We look forward to featuring all of them at our own family get-togethers.

We're especially appreciative to our friends who have allowed us to share their stories. You've made us laugh as we worked, and our book would not be what it is without your tales. Special thanks to Jim Gatling, who received a call from an unknown crazy lady who read his hilarious post from a share on Facebook and researched until she found him. He was gracious enough to say yes when I asked if we could use his story in this book.

I (Michelle) am grateful to my husband, Paul, for always being my encourager and for praying me through each book project. He's the best!

Thank you to Post Hill Press and all the team for being on this journey with us. It's a joy to work with you. And many thanks to Frank Breeden of Premiere Authors for being such a great agent.

We are grateful to Joseph Huntley for the wonderful graphic design work for the cover and for being our friend.

I (Michelle) am so thankful to have had this opportunity to write *Our Daily Biscuit* with my dear friend. Todd and I met at a writing conference many years ago. We both speak Southern, and a lasting friendship was born. I like to tease him that he's the brother I never wanted—but am glad I have. My husband and I love him like family.

We'd be remiss if we didn't tell you, our readers, how much we appreciate you taking the time to read *Our Daily Biscuit*. We hope it is a blessing to you. (And if you want to tell a thousand of your nearest and dearest friends about it, we won't be the least bit upset.)

Finally, last but definitely not least, we are so grateful to God for opening doors for us and for giving us the ability to write for Him. It's our hope that our words will please His heart and touch yours as well.

Todd and Michelle